Beyond the Seventh Gate

Exploring Toad Road, The Seven Gates of Hell, and Other Strangeness in York, Lancaster, and Adams Counties

written and illustrated by
Timothy Renner

with photographs by the author and
A.E. Hoskin

BEYOND THE SEVENTH GATE

Copyright © 2016 Timothy Renner

All rights reserved.

CreateSpace Independent Publishing Platform

ISBN: 153538333X
ISBN-13: 978-1535383332

DEDICATION

to Alison, Gideon, and Ursula
who endure my fascination with all things strange.

to Anthony, Jackson, and David who walked the weird roads with me.

THANK YOU

Brian Magar for photo editing and design help.

Prydwyn for proofreading ... and everything.

Loren Rhoads / *Morbid Curiosity* magazine. My Hex Hollow story originally appeared in Morbid Curiosity #4 (2000). I have modified the original story for this book. I believe Loren was the first person other than myself to ever publish my writing.

Jeff Hilsmeier and the Hilsmeier Family.

Bob Chance very graciously allowed me to peruse his large file of personal bigfoot sighting reports and to photograph casts he has made of locally found footprints.
His help, as well as his patience with the author, has been immense.

Rick Fisher and Lon Strickler, for research help and advice.

BEYOND THE SEVENTH GATE

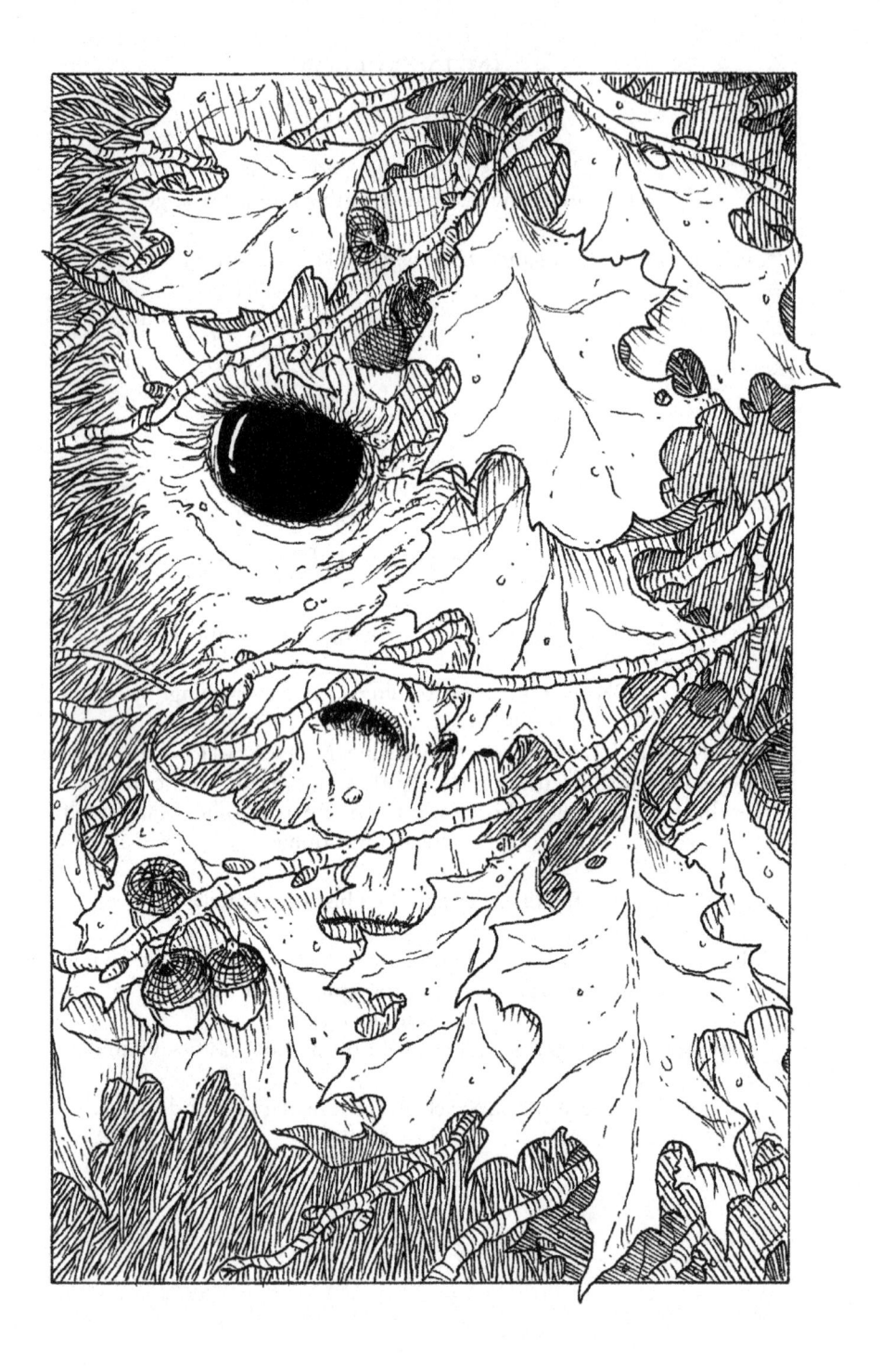

CONTENTS

	Introduction	vii
	Preface	xiii
1	So Where Are the Seven Gates of Hell?	1
2	On Burning Asylums and Mad Doctors and Such	2
3	Hex Hollow History and Mysteries	13
4	Exploring Hex Hollow	25
5	Visiting the River Witch	30
6	Prospect Hill History and Mysteries	36
7	Exploring Prospect Hill	43
8	Toad Road	46
9	Codorus Furnace History and Mysteries	61
10	Exploring Toad Road	67
11	So Where are the Seven Gates of Hell (again)?	81
12	The Albatwitches and Chickies Rock	83
13	Erd Lichtes, Spooklights, and UFOs	91
14	Bigfoot Creatures	100

15	Hex Country Werewolves and Black Dogs	117
16	Flying Phantoms, Mothman, and Thunderbirds	125
17	Jersey Devils, Goatmen and What-Is-Its	132
	Afterword: What to Make of it All	138
	Appendix I: Bigfoot and Other Cryptid Sightings and Signs By Date	143
	Appendix II: Maps	151
	Bibliography	157

photo credits: AEH = A.E. Hoskin. TR = the author. All others noted beneath the image.

A note about the illustrations: These images are meant to be interpretations of the scenes as opposed to accurate representations. Artistic license was taken.

INTRODUCTION

"Don't look behind you on Toad Road!" - this was the warning, as told to me by my wife (then girlfriend) some 25 years ago. She was relating the story - or a fragment thereof - as she remembered it from the early 1980's when she attended day camp in the area.

There was no "Seven Gates of Hell" and certainly none of the tales of insane asylums or mad doctors that so many would later attach to the Toad Road legend. Although I encountered the 'Seven Gates of Hell' legend around the time that I first moved to the area in the mid-1990's, it was at that time a separate story ascribed to Rehmeyer's Hollow in Southern York County, or to Prospect Hill Cemetery in York City.

So how did these legends of insane asylums and mad doctors get associated with Toad Road, and how did the 'Seven Gates of Hell' legend get tied up in the mess as well? Who can say for sure - urban legends are often as much 'whispering down the lane' as they are anything else, and many people tend to not let the truth get in the way of a good story. Still, I have some guesses and I think I can get somewhat close to the matter.

In the late 1990's and early 2000's I was a member of an email discussion group that was made up of legend trippers, ghost hunters, and the like exploring northern Maryland and Pennsylvania legends. Subscribers on this email list included some earnest but ill-researched folks, who were more interested in legends than facts. For instance, photographs of houses built in the 1970's were once presented to the group as Nelson Rehmeyer's house (this was well before the publication of *Weird Pennsylvania* and the many websites which show the actual house). They would frequently change stories and details when confronted with the facts. I don't think there was maliciousness involved - I just think these folks were both excited and excitable and wanted to be the ones who figured out the sources behind the legends. If they couldn't figure out those sources, it seems they had no problem making them up.

I seemed often to be correcting them: No, that is not Rehmeyer's house - how could it be? His murder was in the 1920's and that house was obviously built much, much later. I knew exactly which house was Rehmeyer's, my wife having relatives with adjacent farms. Most of the corrections were just common sense - but some involved a bit more detective work.

As I remember things, it was after one of the legend seekers' weekend trips that they declared on the email list that they had discovered the story of Toad Road and exactly what had happened there. They proceeded to tell a detailed and dramatic story about a burning insane asylum and escaped inmates running through the woods. And here, they said, was where the "Seven Gates of Hell" are found in York County. Alarm bells immediately went off for me. I had never heard of anything like this and I said as much. It sounded like a bad pulp horror story.

It has always been my feeling that folk songs and folk stories - the best ones anyway - contain some grain of truth, some hint of a lesson. Jean Ritchie, the great Kentucky ballad singer, once said "all folksongs are true" - by which I think she meant that there are lessons and truths passed down in these stories. Even if they don't have every fact right, and the names are changed, and the places have slipped from our maps and into some kind of collective folk memory - well, it's still the lessons and the grains of truths that matter. For me, it is this somewhat foggy remembrance of facts, this tenuous grasp of history, that is one of the wonderful things about traditional songs and stories. It is sad, bordering on offensive, when someone is happy just to make up a fiction for the sake of being able to say SOMETHING about a legend. When this happens, we start to lose those grains of truth as they get sifted and lost in the sands of fiction.

My father-in-law has many maps of York County dating back hundreds of years. Nowhere on any of these maps does it show an "insane asylum" on what was Toad Road. Nowhere in any history can you find the mention of an insane asylum in that part of York County. This claim was easier to disprove than it was to make up.

When faced with this on the email list, the tellers of this tale simply changed their story - it wasn't an institutional insane asylum, but a PRIVATE (and sinister) doctor who kept mentally ill patients at his mansion. Further questions made their story morph further with the final version, as I remember it, having moved the location from Toad Road in Hellam Township to Toad Valley Road - all the way down in Shrewsbury (southern York County). I happened to travel regularly on Toad Valley Road, at that time, usually several times each week, and I knew there was no "mansion" there - and certainly no insane asylum. Mostly farmland and farmhouses and barns and a very recent residential development. They seemed to back off on Toad Road after I shot down this last version of their story, and I thought the matter was over.

Some months later I stumbled upon a website purporting to cover legends and mysteries of Pennsylvania. This site reprinted the entire "insane asylum" version of the Toad Road story. I was disappointed, but not surprised.

Fast forward a bit and I am contacted by the *Weird USA* editors. They had read my story on Hex Hollow / Rehmeyer, which originally appeared in *Morbid Curiosity* magazine, and they wanted to reprint it in the *Weird USA* and *Weird Pennsylvania* books. They also asked me to take some photographs for both the Hex Hollow and Toad Road stories they were printing. I agreed to take the photographs but begged them to let me read the Toad Road story before they printed it. I told them there was a lot of made up nonsense about insane asylums and mad doctors and the like.

It was to my horror (and embarrassment) that my photos in their books accompanied some version of the outlandish story I had so easily disproved with a quick look at some maps. In many ways, it's almost too late now - once the story appeared in those books it was like it was canonized in some way and became, somehow, THE Toad Road story. Wikipedia references it and even claims there is no Toad Road. Wrong again. There is, or at least there WAS a Toad Road.

Unfortunately, the fact that Toad Road sits in Hellam Township has made it easy for the "Seven Gates of Hell" to stick to to the place in a bit of urban legend word association. Besides this, that part of Toad Road which was closed off had a gate at the end. A simple metal gate of the type used on farms and such throughout rural America - nothing so grand or fiery as Hell - but it was enough for the email list and enough for *Weird USA*. It's never been enough for me.

There was even an independent horror movie made - both named for and (vaguely) about Toad Road. The film is a bleak and dismal affair, as much about disaffected young adults and drug abuse as it is about the legend of Toad Road, but it further propagated the "insane asylum" story of Toad Road, and further cemented this as THE story in the minds of many.

• • •

When I started this book, it was a simple article about Toad Road and the fallacy of an insane asylum (of any sort) burning on that road. As I pursued the subject I soon realized I was opening those legendary gates, and a lot of high strangeness was pouring through. Even in witch-tales from further abroad in Pennsylvania,[1] York County is noted for its - "hogboblin atmosphere" as are those areas just beyond York County (after all, the paranormal neither abides by county lines, nor stops at the Susquehanna River). These rolling hills and mountains are filled with a history of the wondrous strange which continues even today.

I have been drawn to such things my entire life - ghosts and monsters and Fortean strangeness. My approach for this book has been a combination of documentation and exploration. There is concrete history in some of these stories. Some of it is hard fact. Some things can be proven. In such cases I've tried to be thorough and accurate in my research. Other things are much more ephemeral or liminal (or both). For these things we must rely more on witness testimony - which is easy to discount or disregard, and as regards the veracity of which we must come to our own conclusions. Either the world is full of liars who, for whatever reasons, are making up these tales (often only to face ridicule and derision) - or the world is full of people who have seen SOMETHING strange and odd.

Undoubtably, there are liars and hoaxers among us - as well as cases of misidentification - so there is certainly some grey area in between the two extremes, but for my part I choose to believe most people have nothing to gain from making up a story or perpetuating a hoax. Likewise, I cannot believe that any hoaxer would be dedicated enough to leave

---

[1] see "The Witch of Pine Station" in *Mountain Folks* by Homer T Rosenberger.

thousands of tracks across miles of rural wooded areas in the cold January snow and ice, such as were found in 1978 at Delta in York County.

I don't know that science can adequately answer our questions when it comes to the paranormal. At least not yet. As early as 1973, in his book, *Bigfoot: The Yeti and Sasquatch in Myth and Reality*, Smithsonian primatologist John Napier noted that following these threads can lead one into the "Goblin Universe." The Goblin Universe: that strange dimension coexisting with our own from which these creatures - bigfoot, werewolves, and other monsters - emerge. John Keel's research was already pointing to similar ideas, and *The Mothman Prophecies* would be published in 1975.

If something like the Goblin Universe exists and there are places where the veil between our "reality" and another is thin or parted, then perhaps these haunted and strange places of legend may hold more than mere tales of imagination. Further abroad there is Skinwalker Ranch and the TNT Area outside Point Pleasant to list but two of many - places people consider to be portals to other dimensions - or at least magnets to strangeness in this dimension. Closer to home we have Toad Road, Hex Hollow, and Chickies Rock. If witnesses are to be believed, there are things scarier than ghosts walking through our woods.

So I invite you to come with me as we make our way to places where history and folklore meet in South-Central Pennsylvania - and where, sometimes, creatures step from the folktales and onto the path you have just trodden. Don't look behind you.

• • •

PREFACE:
STRANGE THINGS AND WHAT TO CALL THEM

As I will be reporting and discussing many strange things in these pages, it may be necessary to first speak about the terms I will be using as well as what the book will cover.

Cryptids: A cryptid is any animal which has not been officially documented by the mainstream scientific community. Cryptid creatures include bigfoot, yeti, the Loch Ness Monster et al.

Regarding ghosts: There are many, many books already written about ghost stories from Central Pennsylvania. It isn't my aim to add another full tome to that considerable body of work, so I won't be retelling too many ghost stories in these pages. However, it is simply undeniable that ghost stories seem connected to all of the locales I will discuss, so, where it is relevant or where I believe it is a new or seldom-told story, I will include the tale.

Bigfoot: In general, I use this term to describe any variety of upright-walking, hair-covered hominid. Some researchers have put forth the idea that there may be several different types or species of bigfoot creatures in North America - from the most famous large "wood ape" type as seen in the Patterson-Gimlin film, to others which appear more Neanderthal-like. As this is not a book specifically about bigfoot, we will use the term "bigfoot" to apply to all types, excepting the "dogman" type as noted below.
I use the term "bigfoot" to refer to a species, not an individual, and therefore do not capitalize the word as a proper noun.

Dogman: While many researchers consider "dogman" to be a type of bigfoot, descriptions are different enough to warrant noting it as a separate creature. "Dogman" has become a kind of shorthand for a large, hair covered creature that runs on two or four legs. The legs are sometimes described as "crooked" like a dog's leg - and other times as more hominid-like. The dogman head is described as being like a huge wolf head. This often leads witnesses to describe dogman creatures as werewolves. While I much prefer the term werewolf, that technically describes a human that transforms into the creature. For this reason, I will use "dogman" to describe these creatures.

Goatman: Another unfortunately plain and on-the-nose descriptive name. Goatman creatures have been seen across the country and refer to another upright-walking hair covered creature. This creature is often reported with curved, goat-like horns and sometimes hooved feet.

Mothman: First documented in John Keel's excellent paranormal investigative book *The Mothman Prophecies*, Mothman is a winged, roughly man-sized creature. Sometimes seen flying, and sometimes on the ground, most witnesses agree that the creature is black in color with glowing red eyes, huge wings, and no discernible neck. Sometimes Mothman is described as machine-like, other times as more like a living creature, and sometimes as a shadowy thing that seems to shift between worlds.

Shadow People: Dark, featureless figures, often seen wearing hats. Encounters with a shadow person are almost universally reported as negative, frightening experiences.

• • •

1
SO WHERE ARE THE SEVEN GATES OF HELL?

The short answer is: nowhere. There are not now, nor have there ever been SEVEN physical gates on Toad Road. The Seven Gates, as I was told in the early 1990's, were associated with Rehmeyer's Hollow (Hex Hollow) and/or Prospect Hill Cemetery. I don't believe there were seven *physical* gates in either tale. The way the seven gates were supposed to work - in either story - had to do with driving or walking the roads in the hollow or the cemetery by a certain specific and circuitous route. Each circuit would (symbolically) open a "gate," with things getting progressively worse - presumably more horrible and supernatural - as one passed through the consecutive gates. The seventh circuit or "gate" was to open Hell itself. No one made it to - or at least made it back from - the Seventh Gate.

• • •

2
ON BURNING ASYLUMS
AND MAD DOCTORS AND SUCH

Variants of the Toad Road story tell of an insane asylum that caught fire (or was burned) back on Toad Road - of inmates who perished in the blaze, and also of escaped inmates running through the woods, where some met their end at the hands of angry (or fearful) townsfolk. Other versions tell of a mad doctor who kept dangerous mental patients at his home - patients who later escaped either because of a similar fire or by some other means. Still other versions of the story insist there was a Doctor Belknap, a collector of toads, who lived there, a doctor who so valued his privacy that he put up threatening signs - "if you are found here at night, they will find your body in the morning" and/or "under the sign of the toad, no trespassing". This same doctor apparently loved toads so much that he put up several statues, gargoyles or grotesques that resembled twisted or horrible toad-like things. One wonders, if he loved toads that much why he didn't just get statues of actual toads - not things that sort of resembled horrible toads? There are as many variants of these stories as there are tellers of the tale, but not much evidence for any of them.

There was not ever an "insane asylum" in the area of Toad Road. Some still insist that there WAS an asylum there and that the powers that be in York have done everything they can do to cover up the horrible events that happened there. If this is the case, then the powers that be in York possess some kind of time-traveling and reality-modifying instruments, because they have somehow gone back and changed old maps and literally changed all the history that was ever written down about the subject. It sure would be horrible and spooky if an insane asylum had burned out that way, but on this plane of existence it simply isn't true. There was no insane asylum, therefore there are no ruins of an insane asylum; therefore there are no gates that lead to (or keep folks away from) those ruins. If this is like learning there is no Santa Claus, I apologize, but only briefly. There is plenty of strangeness to go around in regards to Toad Road, and if you'll follow me I will lead the way beyond the Seventh Gate.

• • •

Old maps are lovely things. Before the computer age they were hand drawn and showed everything from residential dwellings to hotels and churches. Hospitals of all types were also shown on these maps.

On the subject of Toad Road itself, there are many different opinions as to where it was (or is) and why it was called Toad Road. Wikipedia and the Hellam Township website both assert that there never WAS a Toad Road, but there is (or was). Northeast of York City, in Hellam Township, and north of the town of Hellam proper, follow State Road 24 north, proceed past Rocky Ridge County Park, and turn on Druck Valley Road - then onto Trout Run Road. Follow Trout Run until its end; where it meets Range Road at an almost 90 degree turn - right there at the corner is the start of Toad Road. You can see the metal gate today. The first and only gate, not one of seven. Toad Road extended Trout Run Road north, through the woods until it met Codorus Creek, and then followed the contours of the Codorus until it met up with Furnace Road - very close to the Codorus Furnace. It's almost as if Toad Road itself was leading to the furnace. Maps dating back to the early 1800's, and possibly before, show Toad Road.

"Moonlight on Codorus Creek" - image from an old postcard.

By the 1940's, this road was being identified as T945 on York County maps, but interestingly so was Trout Run Road; and so was the section of Furnace Road which Toad Road met; and so was what is now River Farm Road (which winds itself around the other side of Codorus Furnace and back through a greater portion of Kondor Woods until it meets up again with Furnace Road further to the east). ALL of this was T945. In the 1940's it was identified as an "unimproved" road - which means, probably, dirt - but by the 1960's T945 is identified as a "graded and drained" road - which means stone. It seems most people can agree where Toad Road started - at the corner of Trout Run and Ridge Roads - but there has been very little talk about where Toad Road ended. Looking at old maps, T945 extended well past and around Codorus Furnace - it was Furnace Road that ended at T945, not the other way around. That said, Trout Run Road was also T945, so the local names of roads didn't necessarily follow the numeration, and vice versa. In online forums discussing the legends of Toad Road, I found comments by posters indicating visits to Toad Road in the 1970's and 1980's (long before *Weird USA/Weird PA* et al.). More than one of these commenters remembered Toad Road as being what is now River Farm Road - this would seem to match with what is shown as T945 on the old maps.

    For now, our attention is with that section of Toad Road which begins at the corner of Trout Run and Ridge Roads. Newspaper articles will be quick to point out that this is private property and trespassers will not be tolerated, so I will echo those statements here. However, Toad Road was not always private property - it was a road, and it was KNOWN as Toad Road even if it never officially bore the name. I have a distinct recollection of a map that identified this section specifically as Toad Road (this is how I found it, after all).

    People seem to have many wild stories (mis-remembrances and guesses, most likely) as to WHY it was called Toad Road - but none of these can be verified. "Toad Road" is not so bizarre a name that the road couldn't have just been named after the animal. After all, there aren't crazy stories about mad doctors threatening to turn people into fish if he caught them wandering on Trout Run Road! To paraphrase Freudian psychology, sometimes a toad is just a toad.

    A more likely explanation for the name, "Toad Road" - whether official or just a nickname comes from a little local driving lore I found in an article from *The Gettysburg Times* in 1989. The article was entitled "Driving Tips for Tourists, Part II" and states: "If you are on a road outside of town just after a rain on a warm summer night, don't be alarmed to see little things illuminated by your headlights hopping in front of you. They're toads. A road with toads is poetically termed by some natives, a *toad road*". The term "toad road" was a descriptive name used by Pennsylvanians to describe roads where toads were often seen.

Back to the maps. No map of Toad Road ever shows a hospital or institution of any kind there. No farms or farmhouses were back there. The only structure ever shown along this section of Toad Road is something marked as a "seasonal or summer dwelling" just north of Toad Road before it meets up with Codorus Creek (between the creek and the road). This was most likely a hunting cabin of some sort. Only as Toad Road becomes Furnace Road do we start to see farmhouses, other occupied dwellings, schoolhouses, and buildings associated with the furnace.

Not only was there not an asylum on Toad Road - why would anyone place an asylum on an unimproved dirt road, or even a gravel road? - but the entire county of York has never really had a specific and dedicated building that housed a mental health hospital. None of the stories about mad doctors and insane asylums on Toad Road ever seem to pin a date upon the events which supposedly happened there. In modern times, there are dedicated floors of York Hospital to mental health, but before 1930 many of the mentally ill in York County would have been sent to The York County Alms House, which was located in downtown York City. Much has been noted on the horrible ways we, as a society, treated mental health patients well into the mid-20th Century, but it is difficult to imagine any circumstances in which a doctor would be allowed to take home and house patients - unless we are talking about a truly mad doctor willing to act outside of the both the law and any sort of doctor/patient morality and code of conduct.

Searching old newspaper articles, there are no notes of fires devastating an asylum or a mansion in the area of Toad Road. You can find many articles on burning mental hospitals -

it did happen, and as close as Philadelphia. These fires were reported in papers all over - not just the local papers. So, again, if the the Toad Road asylum story has been "covered up," the time-traveling agents of York have done a very thorough job - extending their reach beyond the local papers to statewide and possibly even national press! It is as impossible as it sounds.

One of the many online articles misreporting the "facts" about Toad Road and the Seven Gates even shows a photo which they claim is the asylum on Toad Road burning. This photo is in actuality an image of the Brandon Asylum fire from 1910 - this building was located in Manitoba, Canada. Quite a distance from York County, Pennsylvania.

Interestingly, however, there was a building nearby Toad Road, as the crow flies, that was a mansion and a "sanitorium" all in one - and this building did burn to the ground. Just west of the town of Hellam, in 1906, C. Robert Kopp moved into a grand mansion. Kopp had built this mansion with a fortune he made selling snake-oil medicines of his own creation - including his most well known mixture, Kopp's Baby Friend. Presumably "friend" meant "pusher" in this case as Kopp's Baby Friend contained a large amount of morphine. Unfortunately for Kopp, and fortunately for infants everywhere, the Pure Food and Drug act of 1907 forced him to change his ingredients to more subtle treatments such as pumpkin seed and wintergreen oil. His business never recovered. By 1915 he was forced to sell all of his property, including the mansion, for $5.00.

Kopp died alone in a room at the YMCA in York on December 22, 1937, but his mansion still stood. Between 1917 and 1920 it was the home of the Pennsylvania Osteopathic Sanitorium (not a mental hospital). In 1923 it became a nursing home operated by a "Dr." Crandall (it seems Crandall was tried for practicing medicine and surgery without a license - so, was he a doctor?) - and the mansion became known as Dr. Crandall's Health School. On the morning of November 23, 1949, Dr. Crandall's Health School caught fire due to a faulty chimney. By the afternoon of the same day the mansion was burnt to rubble. No one was killed or injured in the fire. No townspeople came to dispense with patients in the surrounding woods. There weren't even woods surrounding the place. Students from the local high school came to watch the flames and some didn't report to school that day so they could watch the fire - but that is as sinister as things got.

Dr. Crandall's Health School - image from an old postcard

• • •

Other versions of the story seem to want to place all the blame for the Toad Road mystery at the feet of Doctor Harold P. Belknap - who is described in these ghost stories as "eccentric" and someone who would threaten people away from his home.

Dr. Belknap was a prominent member of the York community who served in BOTH World Wars. Dr. Belknap taught at both the University of Pennsylvania Hospital and at Johns Hopkins Hospital in Baltimore. He gave lectures on electrocardiography to the York Medical Club and provided medical care at the Society for Protection of Children and Aged Persons Homes.

Dr. Belknap - WWII newspaper photograph

Starting in 1929, Dr. Belknap did work at the West Side Sanitarium in York, but it should be noted that this was not a mental institution. The word "sanitarium" at this time was applied to any place where people went for medical rest. The West Side Sanitarium, also known as West Side Osteopathic Hospital, was just that - a hospital. Upon his return from the second World War, Dr. Belknap opened a private practice in York. By 1948 Dr. Belknap was a member of the Cardiac and Vascular staff at York Hospital.

Dr. Belknap and both of his wives were well known and very active in many social clubs and charities around York. They are often mentioned in the newspapers of the time. I have found no mention of Dr. Belknap's toad collection - nor any hard evidence of toad or toad-like statuary around the area of Toad Road. Leo Motter's book, *Haunted Places in York County Pennsylvania,* in his chapter on The Seven Gates of Hell, makes mention of a hospital "far back in the hills" known as "Dr. Belknap's Fresh Air Sanitarium." There is zero evidence of such a building ever existing. Neither on the maps nor in Dr. Belknap's well documented and respectable medical career. Also, "far back in the hills" would take you quite a distance away from Toad Road, which skirted the Codorus.

After the death of his first wife, Dr. Belknap married his second wife in December of 1953. As of this writing, she is still alive. The newspaper article on their wedding states that they were to live at "Lee Lodge" on Trout Run Road in Hellam Township. From 1953 to 1977 the Belknaps continued to live their lives - Mrs. Belknap frequently getting mention in the local paper's reporting on bridge tournaments and Dr. Belknap occasionally receiving coverage regarding hospital staff appointments or other business relative to his career. Dr. Belknap was the president of the Rose Tree Fox Hunting Club by the early 1970's. Dr. Harold P. Belknap died in August, 1981.

In short, it seems very unlikely that Dr. Belknap was a sinister eccentric, as he is so often portrayed in the books of ghost stories and local legends. He was involved with the community, and had a long and distinguished career as a medical doctor.

On April 22, 1977 two fires broke out in the woods on Dr. Belknap's Hellam Township property. These blazes were described as "fast spreading woods fires." Fire companies from Hellam and Springettsbury Townships responded, but the fires were controlled and extinguished without much trouble.

• • •

There was another fire near Toad Road in 1988. This blaze was at the Codorus Furnace end of the road. There sat a 2-story wooden building, across from the old ironmaster's house (the ironmaster's house still stands, and is still occupied, just uphill from the furnace). This building was an office associated with the flint mill that was on this site in the 1800's. It was unoccupied at the time of the blaze, which was thought to be the work of vandals. No one was hurt in the fire, but the building was a complete loss. The footprint of the structure can still be seen today - it is used as a parking area by the owners of the ironmaster's house.

Drawing of the flint mill office which burned in 1988. This building was located on Furnace Road, near its intersection with Toad Road.

• • •

So, what we have on Trout Run Road / Toad Road is a perfect storm of real things people remember combined with the general Seven Gates of Hell legend that has been floating around York for decades. As it seems to me, someone remembered Doctor Belknap lived back there - and perhaps he had a gate at the end of his property. Perhaps he even had toad-like grotesques on those gates - though this seems unlikely. Someone else perhaps remembered that he worked at the West Side Sanitarium, and assumed it was a mental hospital. Maybe someone else remembered Dr. Crandall's Health School burning down and noted that it was once called a Sanitorium. Perhaps someone else remembered the fires on Dr. Belknap's property in 1977, or the fire at the flint mill office in 1988. Dr. Crandall's Health School and The Pennsylvania Osteopathic Sanitorium were probably mis-remembered and assembled into the nonexistent (and never existing) Dr. Belknap's Fresh Air Sanitarium. It's easy to see this all adding up in someone's mind to the "real" story of Toad Road.

In June of 1972 Hurricane Agnes came to York County. The damage from the storm was considerable, with high water marks still noted on many buildings in local towns. The Codorus Creek flooded West York, washed out various bridges and roads, and left an incredible amount of destruction in its wake. Toad Road - the section between Trout Run Road and Furnace Road - was one of the casualties of the storm. As it was a little-used rural road, it was simply never repaired or re-opened after the storm passed. The land reverted to private property and the now-closed road took on an air of the forbidden, adding to its ongoing spooky reputation.

• • •

3
HEX HOLLOW HISTORY AND MYSTERIES

If you walk the roads in Hex Hollow in the right sequence on Halloween night, you will pass through the Gates of Hell. This is what I was told when I first moved to York County in the 1990's.

Rehmeyer's Hollow, also known as Hex Hollow, is in southern York County, Pennsylvania. It is now adjacent to and includes parts of Spring Valley Park. This county park is sparsely attended, no doubt partially because it's off the beaten path;, and partially because of the rough-hewn roads. But mostly it's because it is Hex Hollow, former home to Nelson Rehmeyer, and location of his "hex house" - where, in 1928, the most famous of Pennsylvania's "hex murders" occurred.

Rehmeyer's Hollow was home to supernatural activity many years before Nelson met his violent end. In the 1800's, Rehmeyer's Hollow was known as Rehmeyer Valley and was already haunted. A story in *The York Daily* from September of 1891 about the general goings on in Rehmeyer Valley notes "the ghost at the lower end of this place has made its appearance again. Several of our people have become so afraid that they will not travel through that place during the night on account of the spook". In 1892 the newspaper notes once more,

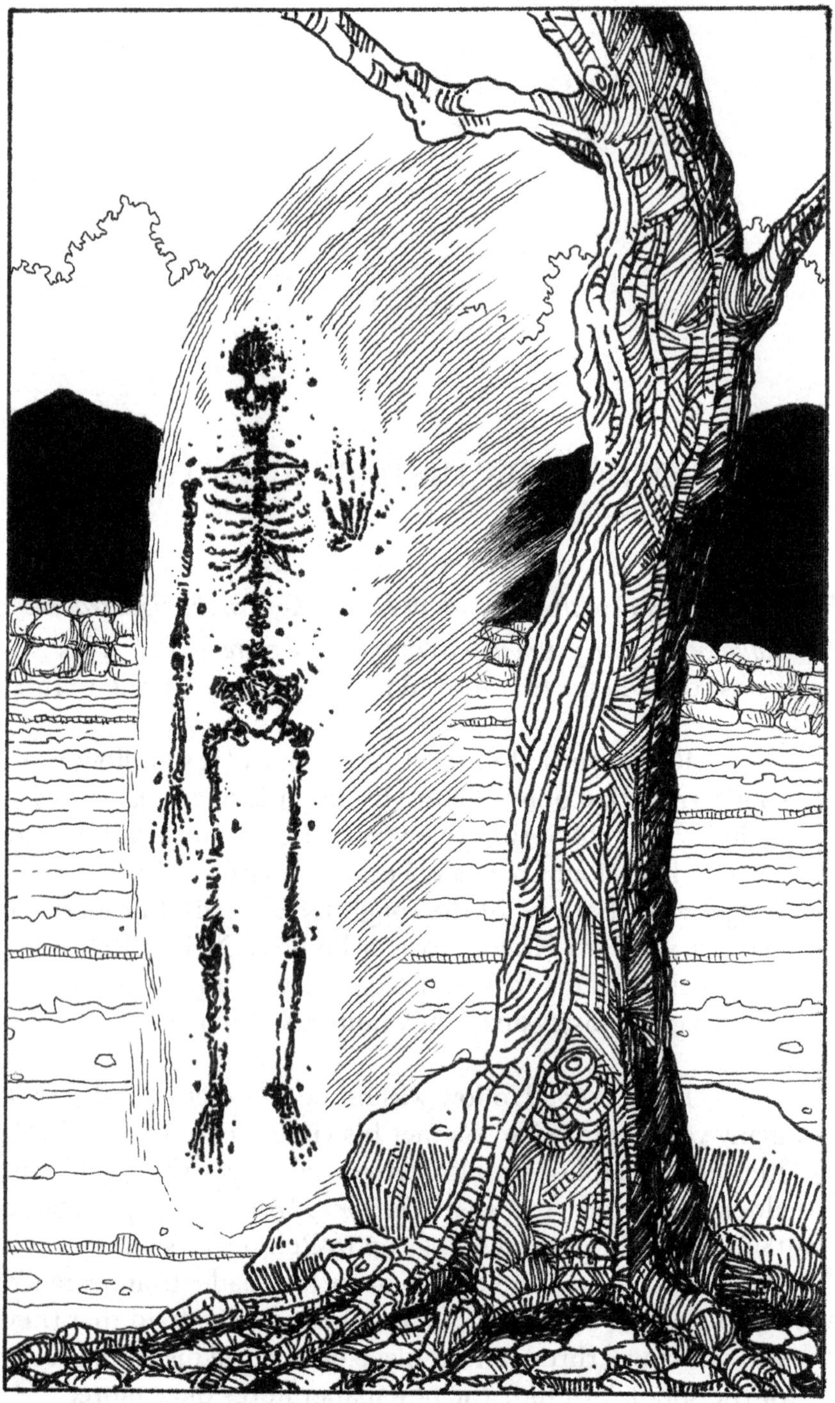

"the spook made his appearance again one night last week in his fiery suit".

However, Hex Hollow is best known by far for the murder of Nelson Rehmeyer. The story of the hex murder, and the trial that followed, were front page news for papers far and wide. Shocking stories of 20th Century "witches" and superstitious countryfolk sold lots of newspapers. Old folk traditions were paraded out as sideshow curiosities, sensationalized, placed out of context, and subject to ridicule. It is around this time that York County began also to be known as Hex County.

In Rehmeyer's Hollow, mazes of trails and rural roads wind around each other. Old fieldstone walls meander aimlessly through the woods. Paths start and end with no particular logic. Sometimes it seems the trees are twisting the roads about, always on the verge of swallowing them back into the shadows. (The East Branch of the Codorus Creek winds through both the park and Hex Hollow. We shall see the Codorus and its various branches wind their way into the stories throughout this book.)

Walking through Hex Hollow, beneath the dark canopy of leaves and reaching branches, it's easy to see how this place could acquire a reputation for witchery even if it wasn't associated with the famous hex murder.

In 1928, the one resident of Rehmeyer's Hollow was Nelson D. Rehmeyer, a loner whose own wife lived outside the hollow because he was, in her words, "too damn peculiar". Rehmeyer stood over six feet tall, with deep set eyes and a powerful presence.

Another Hex Hollow tale I remember: *There is a lonely grave in Hex Hollow, marked with a pentagram, where Nelson Rehmeyer, a black magician, is buried.*

In recent, revisionist, history mostly told by fundamentalist Christians and sensationalists, Nelson Rehmeyer is often called a witch, a necromancer and a black magician. The reality is, he was none of these things.

Rehmeyer was what in York County was most commonly called a powwow doctor. They are also called Brauchers. In a more negative light, they are called Hexenmeisters, Hex doctors, or simply Hexers. While this practice is frowned upon by many Christians - and called Satanic by others - the powwow doctors themselves would never consider themselves evil or witches.

The most common resource for every powwow doctor was a book, *The Long Lost Friend*. *The Long Lost Friend*, more accurately translated as "The Long Forgotten Friend," was written/compiled by John G. Hohman in 1819. It remains in print to this day. Subtitled *A Collection of Mysterious and Invaluable Arts and Remedies Good for Man and Beast*, *The Long Lost Friend* collects prayers, folk magic, superstitions, and rituals that derive from sources as diverse as Gypsy magic and lore, ritual magic, and German folk spells. Hohman himself was a Catholic. That was rare in the Pennsylvania German stronghold of Protestantism, but it didn't make him a "witch".

Neither were the vast majority of powwow doctors. These were men and women who practiced a form of faith healing which they believed to be in line with, not opposed to, their Christian faith. *The Long Lost Friend* sat beside the Bible in many homes, not in its place.

In fact, portions of *The Long Lost Friend* are dedicated to finding witches and breaking their spells and curses. The distinction between the witch (or hexer) and the powwow doctor was underscored by Phillip Smith, who was interviewed by my mother-in-law, Catherine Diehl, in the 1970's. Phillip Smith, deceased, formerly of Jacobus, Pennsylvania, was the last in a long line of powwow doctors. Most of the taped interview

Nelson D. Rehmeyer - old newspaper photograph.

is filled with Mr. Smith giving examples of "trying" or powwowing for people. However, when asked about Rehmeyer, Mr. Smith replied with this answer: "They said they found his hex book. That was no hex book. That was *The Long Lost Friend*." Clearly, Mr. Smith was drawing a bold line between hexerei, or witchcraft, and powwow doctoring - and he was placing Rehmeyer on the side opposed to witchery.

There is no lonely grave in Hex Hollow. No witch's burial ground. No pentagrams, and few hex signs. Nelson D. Rehmeyer is buried in the cemetery at the Old Sadler's Church, just outside of the hollow. No epitaph. No pentagram. He was not a witch.

Rehmeyer's grave - see, no pentagrams. [TR]

In Rehmeyer's time, powwow was practiced openly and regularly. There were storefront powwow doctors in York City and hundreds of informal powwow practitioners throughout the area. One of these was named John Blymire.

Blymire was, by all accounts, a sickly and sad man. Part of an entire family of Brauchers whose spiritual lineage could be traced back to Pennsylvania's most famous witch, Mountain Mary, John Blymire could keep none of his powwow patients. He was reduced to working in a York cigar factory, with no explanation for his hardship, save perhaps for what to someone of his background would have been the obvious answer: he must have been hexed.

Blymire visited every powwow doctor, witch, and faith healer in the area, trying to get his hex broken. He had no luck until he found Emma Knopp, a.k.a. Nellie Noll, a.k.a. "The High Priestess of Marietta", a.k.a. "The River Witch". After many visits - and payments - to Knopp, she revealed the source of Blymire's curse: Nelson D. Rehmeyer of Rehmeyer's Hollow. Blymire claimed that he handed Knopp a dollar bill and when she handed it back, he saw Rehmeyer's face in place of George Washington's.

Knopp told Blymire that the only way he could break the hex was to get a lock of Rehmeyer's hair and bury it eight feet down - or to burn Rehmeyer's hex book. For years, Blymire had been obsessed with his curse; now he had an answer and quickly enlisted aid.

John Curry was a 14-year-old boy who befriended Blymire at the cigar factory. Curry himself had a life full of hard times: a broken family, an abusive stepfather, poverty. It didn't take much for Blymire to convince Curry that he too was cursed and Nelson D. Rehmeyer was the source.

Wilbert Hess was just 17 and his family farm was failing. The farm had been abundant for years; the family could find no explanation why the crops should fail and the cows not give milk - unless it was a hex. Blymire informed them that Nelson D. Rehmeyer was the source. This shocked the Hess family, who knew Rehmeyer. They had taken young Wilbert to Rehmeyer to be healed (successfully). Wilbert had picked potatoes on Rehmeyer's farm. Still, Blymire was sure of the hex and knew how to break it.

Blymire, Curry, and Hess went to confront Rehmeyer on a dark and rainy November night in 1928. On the way, they visited Rehmeyer's wife, to question her about the man. She told the trio where Rehmeyer lived. How frightened they must have been, walking through the hollow that night. The roads must have been far worse then; the woods denser and deeper.

The Hex House as it stands today. [TR]

They knocked on Rehmeyer's door and the old man invited them in. It is possible that he had heard rumor of Blymire's obsession and played it coy that night. They stayed up late talking of many things, from the weather to farming to powwow. Rehmeyer offered them hot drinks and asked them to stay the night - not exactly the actions of a black magician.

Rehmeyer went upstairs to sleep while the trio slept downstairs. Blymire woke up in the early morning and tried to convince Curry and Hess to go to the basement, where it was rumored Rehmeyer practiced his hexerei. That was the most likely place to find his copy of *The Long Lost Friend*. Curry and Hess wanted none of that. Blymire decided that he hadn't yet established the required mental dominance over Rehmeyer. After Rehmeyer fed them breakfast, the trio left.

They returned the following night. Again, Rehmeyer invited them in. Blymire became agitated and more forceful. It took all three of them - Blymire, Curry, and Hess - to wrestle the powerful Rehmeyer to the ground. "Where is it?" they asked. Rehmeyer said he didn't know what they were talking about. They asked again and Rehmeyer said he would get "it" for them if they let him up. When they did, he handed them his wallet, which angered Blymire even more. A fight ensued, continuing for some time. Eventually, the trio held Rehmeyer down, tied a rope around his neck, and beat him to death with a chair and a block of wood. Upon hearing his death rattle, Blymire exclaimed, "Thank God, the witch is dead."

Even with Nelson Rehmeyer dead and tied, the trio could not muster the courage to descend into his basement to look for his "hex" book. Instead, they decided to burn the body and the house. They poured lamp oil over Rehmeyer's corpse and the floor, set them ablaze, and left.

The Hex House - Rehmeyer's Hollow Road is to the right. [TR]

A full moon hung in the November sky. Blymire looked back at the house to see a shadow walk out of the door and lift into the air.

Rehmeyer's nearest neighbor found his corpse two days later, on Thanksgiving, 1928.

Nelson Rehmeyer's house still stands. The blaze set by Blymire was as incompetent as his other pursuits. The "hex house" is not difficult to find, it stands on a small lot along Rehmeyer's Hollow Road. In recent years the formerly green clapboard siding has been replaced with dark wood - taking the house, I'm told, back to the way it looked in Rehmeyer's time.

• • •

Another legend worth noting here, besides the fact that some will still locate the Seven Gates of Hell in Hex Hollow, is a tale about a circle of stones in the woods of Rehmeyer's Hollow known as the Devil's Circle.

Of special pertinence to our current tale is the WAY in which the Devil's Circle is supposed to work - if one walks around the circle clockwise a prescribed number of times (I'm going to hazard a guess that that number is SEVEN) ghostly hounds are said to appear. However, if one walks around the Devil's Circle counter-clockwise, widdershins in occult terms, the hounds will chase you down and you would never be heard from again - presumably dragging you to Hell through whatever portal (or GATE) from which they entered our plane. This sounds a lot like the way the Seven Gates of Hell were supposed to work, as I heard the tale.

Many strange tales are told of Rehmeyer's Hollow. Most of these are ghostly tales:

- Rehmeyer's ghost roaming the hollow.
- Faceless phantoms pacing the roadside.
- Headless hounds.
- Strange lights or faces seen in the window of the Hex House.

However, there are other, somewhat more concrete examples of Hex Hollow weirdness:

There are many tales of cars stalling in the Hollow - sometimes repeatedly. Cell phones and GPS devices sometimes malfunction. Digital cameras freeze or power down without warning. Sometimes brand new batteries act as if they are drained of power.

Orbs and floating lights have been seen, drifting through the trees. Besides the headless ghost hounds and Hell Hounds of the Devil's Circle, black dogs have been reported in Hex Hollow. All of these strange phenomena we will see again (and again) in this book.

There are also stories of bigfoot creatures stalking the woods here.

• • •

4
EXPLORING HEX HOLLOW

I have been to Rehmeyer's Hollow many, many times. I often hike with my family in Spring Valley Park. I was married in Hex Hollow on Halloween night, 1997. I have been swimming in the not-so-secret swimming hole in the creek. I've been all through the woods here, more times than I can count - but never to search for the Devil's Circle or fiery suited phantoms.

The question as to what exactly were the bounds of Hex Hollow was answered, in part, by those old newspaper articles that called it Rehmeyer Valley. This, to my mind, extends it beyond the Hex House and immediate vicinity, and would include Spring Valley Park and some of the surrounding areas. That's a lot of space in which to hide a circle of stones, not all of it public and searchable. It's a lot of land for a flaming ghost to wander as well, and no one has reported that entity in many years.

When I returned to walk the Hollow as part of my research for this book, I didn't actually expect to find the Devil's Circle any more than I expected there to be seven gates and the ruins of an insane asylum on Toad Road. I tried to go

A chainsaw chain hanging from a post in Hex Hollow. [TR]

looking with fresh eyes though, to wander the paths as if I hadn't walked them before. I tried to see if there was anything that could suggest the Devil's Circle, even symbolically.

What I found in Rehmeyer's Hollow was possibility. The Hex House still stands, marking the site of a horrible crime but sparking the imaginations of legend trippers and ghost seekers throughout the region. Like Toad Road, there are roads and bridges here that have been fenced off and are no longer maintained. Nature is taking back what once were easily travelled roads - and it isn't taking long. Who knows what tall tales will be spun giving reasons for these barricaded roads in 20 years?

A rapidly decaying bridge (over Codorus Creek) on a closed road in the hollow. [TR]

The land here, once worked by Nelson Rehmeyer himself, and wandered by a fiery spectre before John Blymire was even born, has been fertilized by the whispering of ghost stories for a century or more. The waters of Codorus Creek, flowing north; carrying the psychic silt and all the wonder and weirdness on through Seven Valleys where the spooklights shine; cutting through the rolling hills of the county and on into York City where it passes just a few blocks from Prospect Hill Cemetery and the Singing Corpse; flowing onward to meet Toad Road and Codorus Furnace just before its waters become one with the Susquehanna River.

Codorus Creek - image from an old postcard.

The meaning of the name "Codorus" seems to be lost to time. Most historical sources give it as a Native American word - perhaps the name of a small tribe of Susquehannocks. Some early sources have it spelled as "Kothores" - a place-name which occurs in Austria - but giving any meaning to the word and tracing its exact source at this point would be conjecture. The creek has been a driving force in the evolution and economy of York from the time the first Europeans tread these soils. Certainly, it was an important resource for the Native Americans before them as well.

  I started to see a connection in Codorus Creek. Like ley lines, those mystical trackways which cross the land, linking sacred places, standing stones, and eerie haunts, the Codorus seems to flow past many places of interest in this book - including all three locations where the Seven Gates of Hell were said to stand. Is it only a coincidence or does the Codorus also flow through the Goblin Universe?

Another closed road in Hex Hollow. [TR]

• • •

5
VISITING THE RIVER WITCH

When I first read of Emma Knopp, the River Witch of Marietta, it was in Arthur Lewis' book *Hex*, which detailed the story of the Rehmeyer murder. There was scant information on The River Witch - and for whatever reason her name was in fact given as "Nellie Noll". Some newspaper articles at the time state that Blymire named The River Witch as a "Nellie Moll".

It seems improbable that Blymire didn't know her name - not only had he visited her numerous times before she handed him that dollar bill with Rehmeyer's face on it, but others have reported that Blymire learned powwow from Emma Knopp. This makes sense, traditionally, as the art was passed down from one sex to the other. So, was he trying to save his teacher from getting involved in the criminal cases that followed by providing a false name? If so, it did not help. With a title as grand as The River Witch, it wasn't hard for newspaper reporters to track her down.

Emma Knopp was born Sarah Emma Attle in 1851 (or thereabouts - some accounts list 1852, 1855, or 1856 as her birth years). In 1860 she was living with her parents just down the road from Marietta in Columbia, PA. She married John Knopp, who worked as an enameler at an iron works, in 1891. John and Emma Knopp lived at 126 East Front Street in Marietta, Lancaster County, PA. She became a widow on July 4, 1918, and continued living on Front Street until her death.

Front St, Marietta - the house where the River Witch died is on the left. [TR]

Newspapers from 1929 report that Emma, then in her 70's, looked much older than her years, with "one sharp tooth," a wrinkled face, and an overall appearance befitting any storybook witch. When questioned about John Blymire, she denied knowing him. Not much else is known about the life of The River Witch - but there is a very interesting story from the New York Times, January 31, 1878, reprinted here as it read then:

Another Pennsylvania Story.

In this, the nineteenth century, it is difficult to believe that the story of a woman being under the influence of a witch would gain a moments credence. Yet such is the case. The little borough of Washington, three miles below Columbia has for several weeks been in a furor of excitement over the story that a woman in that place is bewitched and under the influence of evil spirits. And the excitement is not confined to Washington, but extends to all the neighboring towns. Lawyers, doctors, ministers, and in fact, all classes of people have flocked to see her and many who went into the house disbelieving the whole story, came out firmly convinced of its truth.

The story, as told by the woman herself, will be given below. She lives in a frame dwelling at the extreme end of the borough, and is now confined to her bed. She says that some weeks ago a child, who worked for her, was taken sick in her house, and they did not know what ailed it. A witch-doctor in Marietta was consulted, and then they returned home. The next day a cake was found on a chair in the kitchen, which the woman threw into the stove. The day after a bottle containing some strange liquid was found on the same chair, and this was put carefully away, to be produced in case anything went wrong. The next day a piece of rock-candy was found on the chair, and it shared the fate of the cake. But now the mysterious part began, for when search was made for the bottle of liquid it could not be found, and the conclusion was that it was spirited up the chimney. Several other bottles were found on the same chair, but no matter how they were hidden, they were sure to disappear.

After these demonstrations the woman began to be troubled. Cats were heard crying all around the house, and sounds of a woman in distress. This continued for some time, and then she consulted the Marietta witch-doctor, who gave her some preparation which was to be burned in the stove at night. The preparation was taken to the house, and a young man took on himself the responsibility of burning it. Several persons wished to be present at the burning, but they were told that they would have to stay all night, as it would not do to open the door, for in that case the burning witch might escape. The preparation, which strongly resembled, both in appearance and odor, chloride of lime, was burned, but no beneficial results were apparent.

On the next day the woman began to get worse, and the evil spirit made itself felt. A hand would grasp and throw her to the floor. At first the hand would be as cold as ice, but in a few seconds it would become burning hot, and would leave a reddish brown mark, resembling a burn. This hand sometimes would choke her until she was black in the face, but in every case the marks would be left. This continued until her body was covered with the marks, which a lively imagination could form into figures, letters, prints of hands, reptiles, etc.

At last she became so weak that she was compelled to take to her bed, where she has been for the past two weeks. Some of the clutches, or "grabs," as she calls them, were so fierce that the whole imprint of the finger-nails was left in the flesh. At these times she says that terrible pains shoot through her body. At one time her sight and hearing were entirely gone, but she recovered these senses. Then for a time she was partially insane, and has not yet entirely recovered her reason. Soon after she took to her bed she saw a fiery hand before her face, and after that two balls of fire at the window. One night a black cat jumped against the window trying to force an entrance. Noises, such as sticks being rattled together, horses tramping on the porch, etc, were heard every night. A few weeks ago a hog died on

THE PREMISES AND ITS DEATH WAS ATTRIBUTED TO WITCHCRAFT.

A PHYSICIAN WHO EXAMINED HER GIVES HIS OPINION THAT THE MARKS CAME FROM A SKIN DISEASE. SHE HAS BEEN SUBJECT TO EPILEPTIC FITS SINCE HER CHILDHOOD, AND DURING THESE FITS IT IS VERY PROBABLE THAT SHE WOULD CATCH HOLD OF HER OWN PERSON WITH A CONVULSIVE GRASP, AND THIS WOULD ACCOUNT FOR THE MARKS OF FINGER-NAILS IN HER FLESH.

Could the witch-doctor mentioned in this article have been a young Emma Knopp? Or the person who schooled Emma in powwow? How many witch-doctors, powwow doctors, and witches were in Marietta?

Emma Knopp died March 28, 1933, taking the answers to many mysteries with her. At the time of her death she lived at 124 West Front street, just a few doors down from the haunted Shank's Tavern. She is buried in Marietta Cemetery on West Fairfield Avenue, Marietta. I have been, as yet, unable to find her grave - but I keep searching.

• • •

Marietta Cemetery - somewhere herein lies Emma Knopp. [TR]

6
PROSPECT HILL HISTORY AND MYSTERIES

Prospect Hill Cemetery in York City proper was the other home to the Seven Gates of Hell as I was told so long ago. The main entrance gates are on North George Street (the building at the entrance is called "The Gate Lodge" - if you are keeping track of "gate" synchronicities as we move along), but this sprawling graveyard has quite a collection of corpse roads to drive about, to wind around, including several circles and even graves laid out in circles. If one wanted to devise a circuitous route - a route that involved graves and spookiness and lots of actual gates - one could do worse than Prospect Hill. Just out of curiosity, I looked up a Google satellite image. Guess how many entrances to Prospect Hill Cemetery the satellite shows? Seven. I am including service entrances and what may be walking paths - but seven ways in (or out) of Prospect Hill. There are actual GATES as well - at least seven - but who knows how many were there whenever the legend of the Seven Gates was initially started - and how many have been changed, removed, or added since then? I'm speaking only of entrance gates here, and not of gates into family plots or mausoleums - of which there are a few within Prospect Hill.

The Gate Lodge at Prospect Hill Cemetery. [AEH]

People were being buried at Prospect Hill as early as 1835 - before it was an official cemetery. Before that, it was an orchard. Prospect Hill became an official cemetery in 1849. This 170 acre necropolis is well kept and makes a nice place to walk and find some graves of interest - both in terms of memorial sculpture and local historical figures. The oldest part of the cemetery was laid out in circular plots to allow horse drawn hearses and carriages to more easily navigate the roads. Having expanded greatly during the time of motor cars, the bulk of the cemetery now has straighter lanes that criss-cross throughout.

Though free from the more horrible cryptids and stalking creatures we find at other locations throughout this book, Prospect Hill does have its own glowing-eyed entity, the Singing Corpse.

Monument of Delilah Burnham at Prospect Hill. Burnham was a local actress, married to the owner of the York Opera House. [AEH]

In 1902 a power company employee was working on the street lights in the pre-dawn hours near Prospect Hill Cemetery. He heard a voice of "angelic sweetness" singing the old hymn, *Nearer My God to Thee*. Looking around for the source of the song, he saw a figure standing in the cemetery beside a dark mound crowned with a marble headstone.

The eerie figure of a man was well-dressed in a black suit, one hand resting upon the tombstone, the other holding his hat by his side. His face was pale and gaunt. His bloodless lips formed the words of the hymn. The lampman fled - running at full speed for the safer environs of York City, where he was found breathless and shaking in fear.

In the nights following, many who passed by Prospect Hill Cemetery reported on the ghostly serenader. The haunted strains of *Nearer My God to Thee* drifted amongst the tombs. Streetcar operators and pedestrians reported seeing and/or hearing the strange nocturnal figure.

Hearing the tale of the singing spectre, two curious and skeptical men from York decided to spend the night in Prospect Hill Cemetery in order to get to the bottom of the mystery. Harry Metzel and George Adams decided they would even go so far as to confront the man, be he ghost or mortal. On the night of April 4, 1902, Metzel and Adams made their way to Prospect Hill Cemetery.

In Harry Metzel's own words: "I've never placed any stock in ghosts, and my friend Adams is not over credulous. When I asked him if he would be afraid to spend a night in the cemetery with me to watch for the singer, he said he thought that no harm could come to us in a place that is peopled with the dead, and readily agreed to accompany me.

"It was 11:30 pm when we entered the cemetery by scaling the fence. The spot where the singer appears had been pointed out to me on a previous morning. Under a pine tree

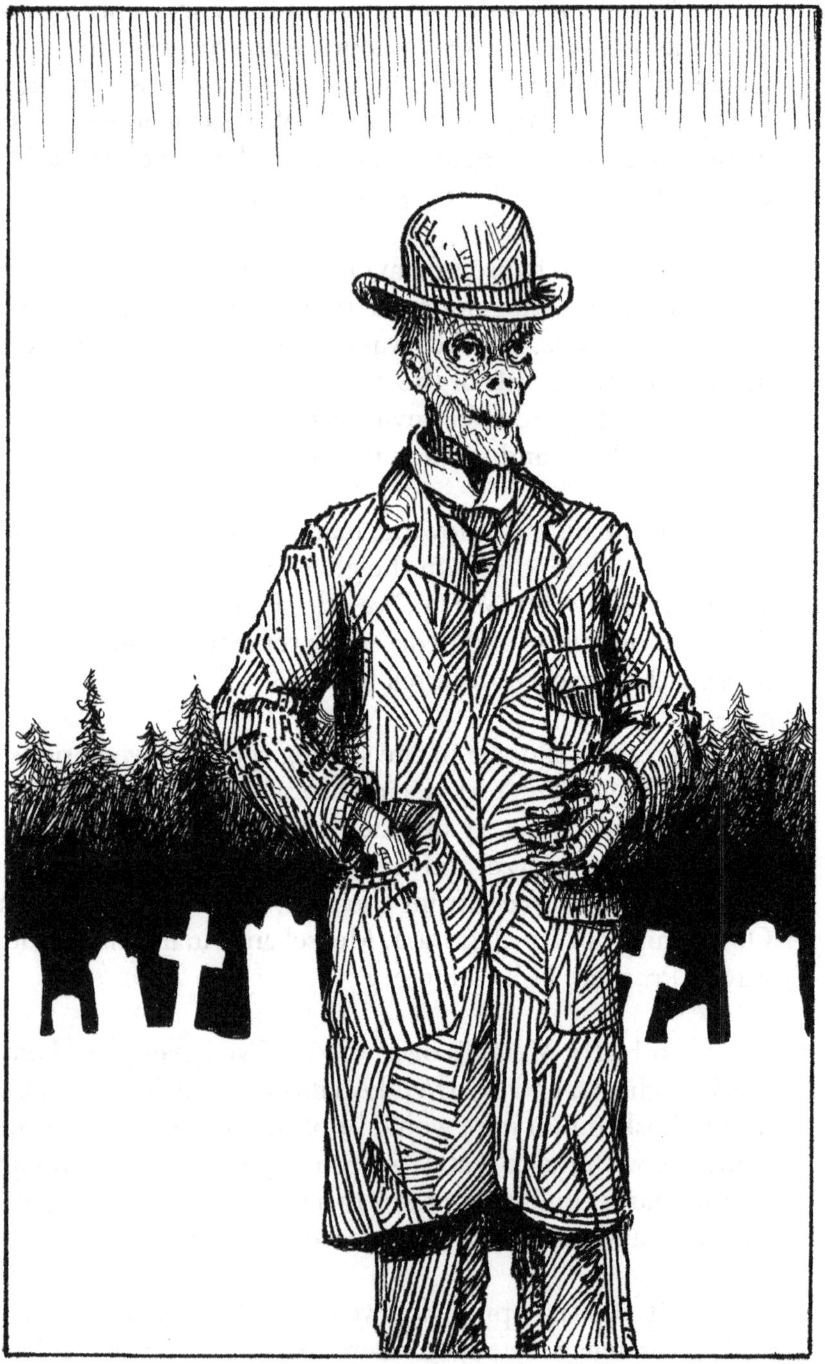

about fifty rods from the spot we found a rustic seat, which we occupied. An hour passed without incident, and we had become so engrossed in conversation that we had quite forgotten the object of our visit to the lonely place.

"Suddenly, Adams, who was talking, ceased, and clutched me by the arm. 'Look!' he exclaimed - and following the direction indicated by his pointed finger I saw, standing at a graveside with his back toward us, a well-built man, somewhat above the medium height and attired in a dark suit. Neither Adams or myself had observed how the man or apparition, for now I am not certain which of these it might have been, reached the graveside. My heart was beating ragtime, and I could hear Adams's heart bumping against his ribs, when a sweet, clear voice, the like of which I have never heard before, echoed through the trees. It was the singer, sure enough, and he was singing *Nearer My God to Thee*.

"Enraptured, we both listened. We could not move - our limbs seemed to be paralyzed. When the singer concluded the last verse of the hymn I regained enough of my courage to find my voice and I shouted, 'Hello there! Who are you?' Slowly the figure wheeled about and we saw a face of deathly pallor and a pair of eyes that were glowing like live coals, fixed upon us. That was enough for us. We made a dash for the fence and how we ever managed to scramble over it I am at a loss to know. Had a band of wild Indians been at our heels, we could not have made better time in reaching York.

"Are we going to watch again? No, thank you. Once is enough for us. So far as we are concerned the singer can have Prospect Hill Cemetery all to himself any night he wants it. If the singer is a mortal he is wasting his time singing in cemeteries, for his voice would bring him a fat salary in a church choir."

• • •

Was this the old evergreen under which Metzel and Adams sat waiting for The Singing Corpse? The author stands beneath the tree. [AEH]

7
EXPLORING PROSPECT HILL

Prospect Hill differs a bit from other locations in this book in that it has quite literal boundaries. Much of it is marked by stone walls or fences; lines of trees or side streets. I wouldn't have to wander the woods, wondering if I am even near the right place as was the case with the Devil's Circle, which I doubt is really even in Hex Hollow.

Whichever grave The Singing Corpse stood upon had to be in the older section of the cemetery - that section toward the front with the circular roads. With the number of graves in Prospect Hill, finding where the Singing Corpse sang his hymn might be like looking for a needle in a haystack, but there were some clues. I thought I would look.

The lampman noted the undead singer stood upon a dark mound masked by a marble headstone 20 rods from the fence. A somewhat archaic measurement, a rod is 5½ yards - which places the Singing Corpse about 110 yards from the fence. While there is no fence these days, old photos show it stood where the stone wall stands today.

Our brave ghost hunters, Metzel and Adams gave further clues indicating they placed themselves some 50 rods (275 yards) from the grave where The Singing Corpse appeared, under a pine tree. The hills and trees around Prospect Hill don't allow for too many places were this could be: a pine tree, old enough to have been there in 1902, with a view of graves 275 yards away. Of course, all parties involved were estimating the distances and could well have overestimated - but taking them to be close, I found just a few pine trees which may have been candidates for the place Metzel and Adams found their "rustic seat".

Graves at Prospect Hill Cemetery. [AEH]

I thought perhaps finding the grave upon which The Singing Corpse was standing might give a clue to his identity. It was not to be. As in my search for Emma Knopp's tombstone, I was left wandering the graves on a grey day. Prospect Hill itself is beautiful and peaceful. The green of the grass and the trees make it seem as much a park as a cemetery. There are worse places to wander.

At night I pass by and listen for strains of *Nearer My God to Thee*. I hear nothing but the noises of the city. A few blocks away the Codorus makes its way toward Hellam. I wonder if The Singing Corpse walked that way as well.

• • •

8
TOAD ROAD

The greatest portion of the Toad Road legend has, at least in recent years, been taken up by the burning insane asylum / Seven Gates of Hell story popularized by *Weird USA* / *Weird Pennsylvania*, Wikipedia, the eponymous film, and even Hellam Township's own website. As I believe I have already addressed (and dismissed) these versions of the story, I won't pay too much attention to them here, but instead concentrate on the strange phenomena people have experienced - and the strange things they have seen.

Before entirely abandoning the Seven Gates, however, it is worth considering one aspect of the stories of some who claim to have walked Toad Road - the feeling, and sometimes the experience, of things getting stranger or scarier the further one proceeds. I believe this is what most people mean when they say they have been "past the fifth gate" or something similar. If they are not talking metaphorically, they were either at a different location which they *believed* to be Toad Road or they are lying, because there aren't seven physical gates.

Toad Road - the gate in winter. [TR]

When walking Toad Road from the gate at the corner of Trout Run and Ridge Roads, every step leads you deeper into the woods. Every step leads you closer to Codorus Creek. If there are things in the woods waiting for you, every step is more dangerous than the last. If you are brushing against, or even walking into the Goblin Universe, the longer you are there, the stranger things will get. It may begin to feel very much like you have passed through a gate and into a very different place.

For every person who claims to have walked Toad Road and experienced something, there are many more who say they have been there with nothing happening. This neither proves nor disproves anything - each person's experience is bound to be different. Any event that happens on a single day - be it mundane or paranormal - may not necessarily be repeated on any other day. If your friend is out for a walk in the woods and tells you he saw a bluebird in a particular tree, you could walk the same trail a week, a day, or even a few minutes later and the bluebird may or may not be there.

The Codorus Creek - view from Toad Road. [TR]

There are, however, many witness reports of strange things on and around Toad Road - from eerie ghostly forms to strange sounds and more. I have done my best to filter out any experiences which were coupled with statements such as "I found the foundation of the burnt asylum" (no, you didn't). Stories which were tied too obviously to the insane asylum myth, I have tried to eliminate.

One of the most frequently occurring elements of Toad Road stories is screams from the woods. Most often described as a "woman screaming", those looking to confirm the burning insane asylum story of course claim such screams to be made by the ghosts of the asylum victims. However, what else screams in the woods?

Foxes scream. Owls screech. Rarer, but still sometimes reported in Pennsylvania, wild cats can scream. On two consecutive days in 2006, I saw a cougar in a field in northern Maryland, just below York County - something which is absolutely not *supposed* to be there, but which most certainly was. All of these things, even the cougar, fall within the realm of the natural, but there is something else that is said to scream in the woods.

Bigfoot. The screams have been reported - even recorded - from all over the USA and Canada. Notable features which seem to distinguish bigfoot screams from others mentioned above are the volume and the sustain of the screams. Those who have heard the alleged hominid howls in person say they are much louder and much longer than other animal screams and screeches. It's difficult to tell the volume on the recordings, but the sustain is evident. Those features match up with what witnesses describe on Toad Road. Loud screams - sometimes so loud they hurt the ears. Sustained howls - screams that carry on and on.

Still, you may think that ghosts are as reasonable an explanation as bigfoot, given that we have placed one foot in the Goblin Universe. That is true, however the woman's screams call to mind yet more bigfoot reports. Reports regarding other cries and screams in the woods.

Almost every Native American tribe has some version of bigfoot. Wild men of the woods, stone giants, windigo, gugwe, omah - the list is quite long. Many of the Native Americans' stories do not paint these creatures as gentle giants of the forest. They are often portrayed as people snatchers. Sometimes even people eaters.

You do not have to go far down the rabbit hole to find modern tales of bigfoot stalking and of aggression toward humans. What you will find in many of these stories are screams, sounds like crying babies (also reported on Toad Road), and sometimes even mimicry of human language from the bigfoot creatures. Humans are both naturally curious and inclined to help other people who are in trouble - particularly those we see as helpless. It may be one of the great factors in our survival as a species. What better way to draw humans out into the woods than the sound of a baby in distress?

Bigfoot are also well noted for pacing people in the woods. Staying just out of sight in the foliage, but moving parallel through the trees. Many, many hikers and hunters have noted this behavior in their bigfoot encounters. The reader will see it again near Holtwood Dam in York County in Chapter 14. Likewise, on Toad Road more than one witness has described being paced by *something*, just out of sight.

"Don't look behind you on Toad Road!" We return to that first fragment of a Toad Road story I heard way-back-when, remembered by my wife. She herself learned it at her day camp off of Jerusalem School Road - which somewhat parallels Toad Road, on the other side of Codorus Creek. She remembers a person pointing in the direction of Toad Road as they gave her the eerie warning.

It's an ominous enough phrase on its own, suggesting stalking behavior by WHATEVER or WHOEVER might be behind you. The phrase bounced around in my head for years and years. I didn't exactly know what to do with it or how it fit into the Toad Road story. Then I stumbled upon The Hidebehind.

Robert R. Lyman was a collector of Pennsylvania folklore and stories of strange creatures. He collected many tales from the 1600's through the 1970's. He tells of a creature

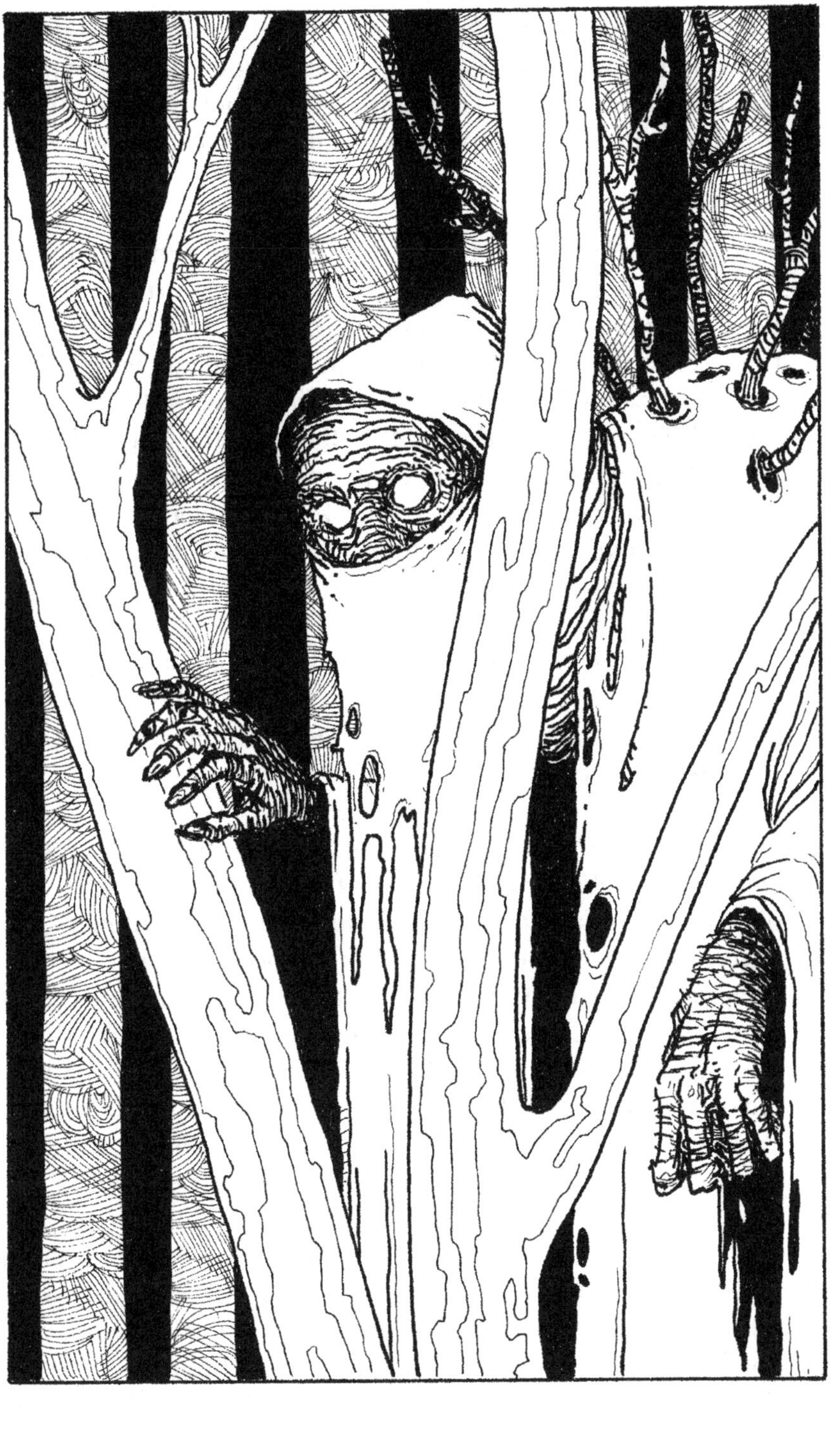

known to local Native Americans called The Hidebehind. It was said to follow people through the woods, always behind its victims, hiding behind trees and peeking out from them. It is worth noting that tree-peeking is another well known bigfoot behavior.

The Hidebehind was not the shy and retiring creature its name would suggest, but the most feared entity in the Pennsylvania forest. It was said that, when traveling through the woods, the bravest person should be the last in line. Only the bravest could be relied on to *never look behind* as they walked. To look behind would spell doom, for The Hidebehind creeped in their wake. Should anyone turn to see The Hidebehind they would be struck with fear and panic and the creature would surely take them. When The Hidebehind takes someone, they are never seen again.

There it was. "Don't look behind you." The Hidebehind, creeping from the pages of folklore and into the woods of York County. Still stalking the wilds of Pennsylvania. Still inspiring fear on Toad Road.

The Hidebehind also calls to mind another very sinister connection. *Missing 411*, a series of very interesting and disturbing books by David Paulides, deals with strange disappearances of people. Most of his books tell of disappearances from national parks or other wilderness areas. Many of the disappeared are never seen again. Paulides identifies clusters of missing people from specific geographic areas. Yosemite and the Great Smokey Mountains National Parks contain two of the biggest clusters, for instance. The *entire state* of Pennsylvania is noted as another cluster.

Those that are found, alive or dead, are often found in very strange circumstances. Toddlers, for instance, are found miles and miles away from where they went missing, through impossibly dense wilderness or up steep mountains even experienced climbers would have trouble scaling. Bodies of the missing are sometimes found placed in the middle of trails which have previously been walked and searched many times.

Paulides has noted many odd commonalities among the cases he has profiled. There are two worth noting for our purposes. First, the cases of the missing occur disproportionately in places with the words Devil or Hell in their name. Devil's Doorway; Hell Run; Big Devil Swamp; Hellgate Mountain; the list goes on and on. In this book we have already searched for the Devil's Circle and The Seven Gates of Hell. Second, Paulides notes that the missing are often the *last in line* if they were traveling in a group. The Hidebehind strikes again.

I should note that Paulides, to his credit, is very careful not to suggest what exactly is taking people in the woods or elsewhere. He only reports, noting any strange details and coincidences between the cases. He never concludes that bigfoot or aliens or even a human agency is responsible for the disappearances. This may be out of respect for the families. I think it must be difficult enough to suffer the loss of a loved one without people speculating on what took them - especially if you are suggesting something paranormal may be involved.

Taking this into consideration, I shall leave the names out here in respect for the families, but I have found reports of one person who went missing close to the area of Toad Road, and of two hunters who died there as well. The missing person case is relatively recent. She just disappeared and, as of this writing, is still missing. Of the two hunters that have died there, one is assumed to have fallen from his tree stand. The other was found dead after discharging his shotgun twice.

It is very difficult to search for *found* people - that is to say people who went missing but were then found alive - so I can't say how often that has happened around Toad Road. The woods aren't so very deep around Toad Road that one could not just keep walking in any direction and eventually find one's way

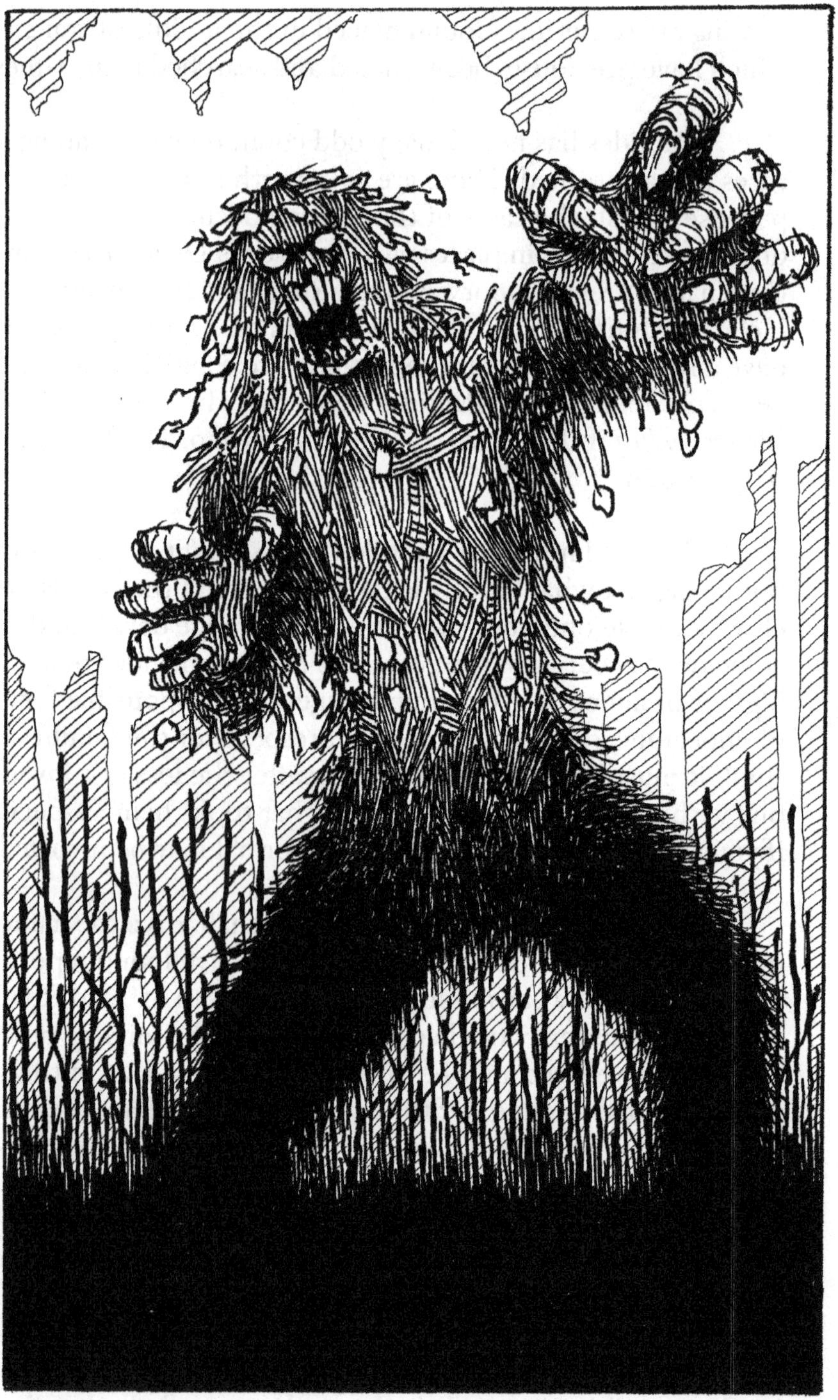

to a road or a house. It seems to me that if someone goes missing on Toad Road, they would have to be taken, not just gotten lost.

So, we have moved Toad Road away from being just a spooky ghost story and into the realm of monsters. What else can we find? How about an actual monster attack? Indeed, at about 5:00 am on December 1, 1973, Michael Findley was attacked by what he described as a "green haired monster" on Trout Run Road. The newspaper account offers no other details except to say the man was admitted to York Hospital to be treated for scratches on his face. The police found no monster.

A green haired monster sounds so outrageous it would be easy to dismiss, but one is reminded of the Honey Island Swamp Monster from Louisiana - a bigfoot type creature which was said to have swamp weeds matted in its hair. Other reports of bigfoot creatures give them an almost chameleon-like ability to blend in with their surroundings. Maybe the monster only appeared to be green?

There are also cryptid reports of giant *purple* hairy monsters in other states. Giant purple bat-winged creatures with 40 foot wingspans. What about the upright canines in clothing, smoking cigarettes, as reported near Skinwalker Ranch in Utah? Compared to sightings like these, perhaps a green haired monster is not so outrageous.

Local musician, James Kibler told me a story about an accident on Toad Road involving an unidentified creature. His father, Andrew C Kibler III, was riding a motorcycle on Toad Road in the late 1960's or early 1970's. He encountered an unusual creature on the road. The sighting was so disturbing that it caused him to swerve and wreck. He broke his ankle in the accident. The injury troubled him for the rest of his life. Like so many witnesses to the unusual, Andrew never did give many details on what he saw - he would only tell James it was an animal unlike any other he had ever seen.

Quite a few other witnesses report encounters with dogs on Toad Road. Some of these are the ubiquitous black dogs which we shall discuss more later. These are a most difficult element of supernatural stories, for are such black dogs simply dogs, domestic or wild but wholly natural? Or are they ghosts, or some kind of cryptid thing? It's hard to say, but they do seem to appear again and again in these places of weirdness. Other canid reports on Toad Road suggest wolf headed things and dog heads that appeared "too high" in the trees. This could suggest dogmen or spookwolves prowling the woods.

Bigfoot. The Hidebehind. Green haired monsters. Dogmen. Are they all facets of the same phenomenon? Are they all the same thing - or completely different entities drawn, for some reason, to the area of Toad Road? Are they stalking people through the Hellam Hills? Are these weird things coming out of the Goblin Universe and into our own?

For me, however, finding The Hidebehind took the legend back in time a bit - past the nebulous Seven Gates of Hell associations - and connected Toad Road with a much older aspect of Pennsylvania folklore. It can be proven that there was never an insane asylum on Toad Road. That part is easy - but people still claim strange things happen in the area, and many of those claims seem to have the features of cryptid encounters as opposed to the usually more passive ghost sightings.

Of course, there are still ghost stories tied to Toad Road. Oddly, few have to do with supposed insane asylum victims. Draw from that whatever conclusions you may. The most frequently recurring story seems to be that of a spirit of a young girl which warns people away from the area. Quite a few people say that this spookette met them at the "fifth gate" (or one of the others), which is problematic. These stories I immediately discount, for there is no physical "fifth gate". Other people say the young ghost met them just inside the first (and only) gate. Still others state that the disembodied voice of a young girl calls for help from the woods. Assuming this is not a cryptid creature practicing mimicry to lure its victims, one would guess the voice belongs to the same ghost girl.

In doing my research, I asked almost everyone I knew if they had any strange stories about Toad Road. I was particularly interested in hearing from people who were over age 40 - as they were more likely to remember stories that came before *Weird USA* et al. I was told one story of what may have been a ghost, may just have been a strange man, or may have been *something else* at Toad Road.

Darren Swengel, a resident of York who lived in Hellam at the time, remembers traveling to Toad Road around midnight one Sunday in 1987 or 1988. He and some friends were bored and looking for a thrill, so they set out for Toad Road. As their car passed the corner of Ridge Road and Trout Run Road, they met with a truly eerie sight.

At the time there was a cable between two posts that served as a "gate" / road block. Sitting upon the cable was a man dressed all in white. A white suit jacket. White shirt. White slacks. White shoes. White hair spiked up above a pale white visage. He stared straight ahead and didn't react to the headlights or the passing car. He just continued staring. Five people in the car with Darren witnessed the strange sight. Two of the women in the car began screaming, but still the strange man never flinched. He just sat there, staring straight ahead, with his hands on his knees.

Why was he there? What was he doing sitting on that gate at midnight? By this time, Dr. Belknap would have been dead, so if it was him trying to scare kids away from the area, he was in his phantom form.

Before we leave Toad Road, I must note some very dark things that happened in the area, not by any unexplained sources, but by the hands of humans. There have been several

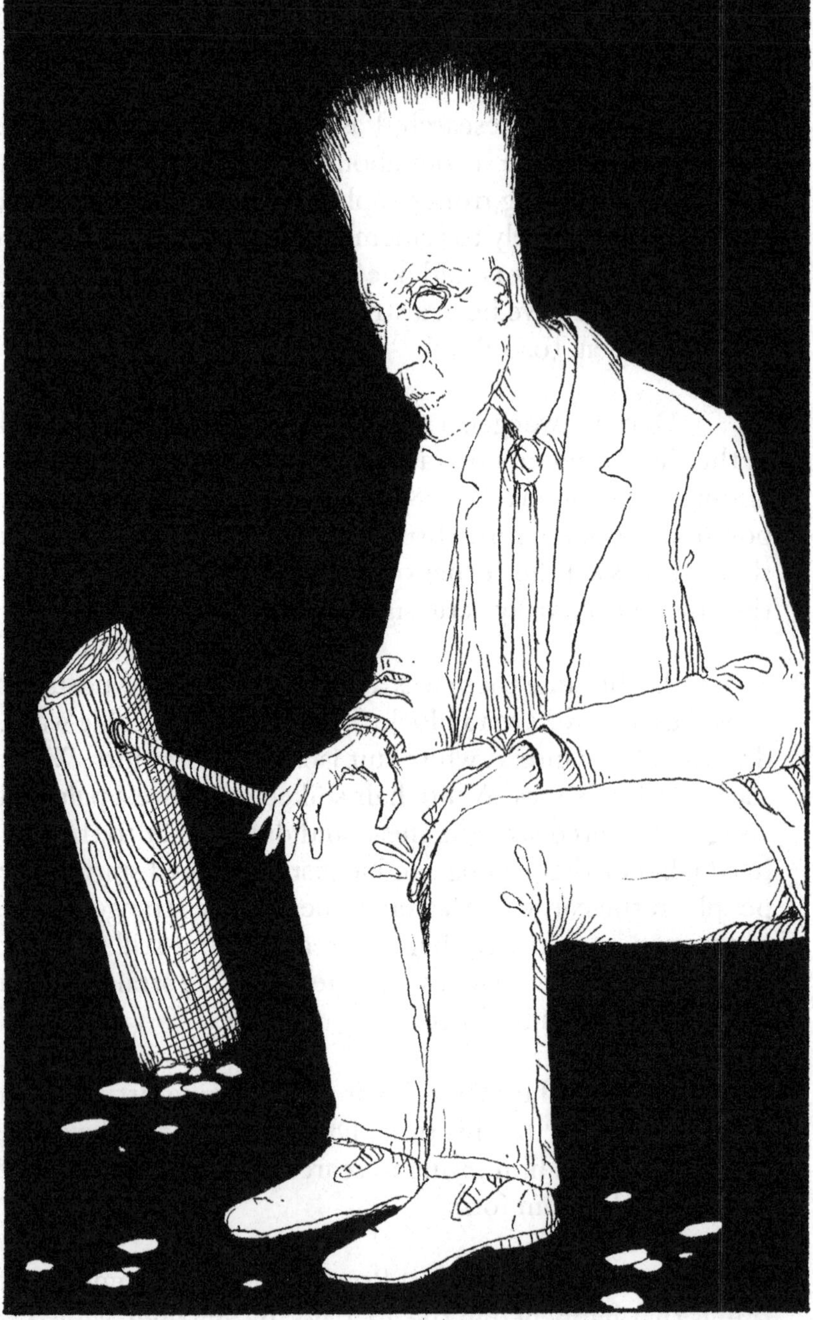

deaths recorded in the area of Toad Road / Codorus Furnace, other than those of the two hunters already mentioned. A burned body of a man was found in the 1950's near Codorus Furnace - an apparent suicide by self-immolation. In the 1970's, multiple bodies were found in the woods here with gunshot wounds. Another man was shot and then had his body thrown in Codorus Creek, wrapped in chains. While not supernatural, these horrible deaths only add to the dark aura of the region. Who knows what psychic scars they have left on the landscape and in the fading memories of locals?

If there is a force that draws supernatural events to areas like Toad Road, does it also, in some way, draw the darkness from men? Were they drawn to this area to do horrible things by some force beyond understanding? Is there a reason those crimes and tragedies happened here, other than the fact that it is somewhat remote? Surely there are plenty of other remote places in the region.

• • •

Toad Road itself. 2016. [TR]

9
CODORUS FURNACE HISTORY AND MYSTERIES

You would be hard pressed to find a historic iron furnace in Pennsylvania that does not have some kind of supernatural tales associated with it. Most often these take the form of ghost stories - the most famous is perhaps the tale of the Eternal Hunter or "der Ewige Jäger".

The Eternal Hunter has been associated with more than one furnace in Pennsylvania, but it is most often tied to Cornwall Furnace in Lebanon County. The tale of the Eternal Hunter tells of a cruel ironmaster who ran his hunting hounds into the fires. The ghosts of the hounds haunted the man unto his death, at which point he remained on earth, in spectral form, to forever roam the hills with his phantom hounds.

While the ghostly tales associated with iron furnaces are well documented, there is little explanation as to why these relics of the earliest stages of the industrial age somehow act as supernatural lightning rods.

The simplest explanation may be that these strange stone towers just LOOK haunted. Their practical use mostly

Codorus Furnace. 2016. [AEH]

forgotten, these relics from another age jut up from the ground as if the earth itself heaved them from its bowels. Then again, perhaps there is some significance in was what was made at the furnaces - many of them supplying the cannons, cannon balls, grapeshot, and other implements of war that would leave death and misery in their wake.

Work at iron furnaces was so dangerous that laws were passed as early as 1726 prohibiting the sale of alcohol at any establishment within two miles of the forges. Many furnace workers were injured or killed. Perhaps these fallen workers have left their spirits at the furnaces - or perhaps it is simply the dark memories that taint the recollections of iron furnaces.

Iron itself works into many supernatural tales. Plutarch noted iron as the bone of the gods. Iron was believed to repel ghosts, fairies, and witches. The iron horseshoe has, of course, long been a symbol of good luck. Ideas of magnetic fields and ley lines tie iron to the supernatural elements within the earth itself. Perhaps then, it is only natural (or supernatural) that these abandoned iron works, no longer working with that metal of good luck - no longer producing the ferric bane of faeries - should draw to them that which it once repelled. To extend the metaphor, it is as if the poles of the magnet were reversed - and now all strange things are attracted to the abandoned iron furnaces, instead of being pushed away. Just within these pages we have the River Witch's husband employed at an iron works, all of the furnaces in Chickies Rock (see chapter 12), and Codorus Furnace.

Codorus Furnace, also known at various times as Codorus Forge, Hellam Iron Works, and Hellam Forge, today stands at the junction of Furnace Road and River Farm Road. In 1765, William Bennet erected the forge on a 150 acre tract obtained from the Penn family. Bennet continued running the iron works until May 21, 1771. At this time the furnace passed into the hands of York County sheriff Samuel Edie, who in turn sold it to Charles Hamilton. Hamilton transferred ownership to

James Smith, one of the signers of the Declaration of Independence. Smith, who would later become a member of the Continental Congress, made cannons and ammunition for the Continental Army during the Revolutionary War at Codorus Furnace.

During the Revolutionary War three top British secret agents were given orders from General Howe to find and destroy "ye military forge at york town" (Codorus Furnace). Two of these agents went missing in their search and were never heard from again. (Perhaps they looked behind themselves while searching the Hellam Hills?)

James Smith found the furnace a losing venture, however, and claimed to have lost $25,000. He blamed the two managers of the iron works. Smith famously said of the managers, "One was a fool and the other a knave." While in Congress, Smith sold Codorus Furnace to a York merchant, Thomas Niel. In 1810 the plant was purchased by Henry Grubb, who expanded the operation. Under Grubb, the furnace would also supply munitions for the War of 1812. One of Grubb's managers was John T. Ubill who later became a slave-catcher, collecting reward money for returning escaped slaves to the south.

In 1837 the Codorus Furnace was partially rebuilt and remained a functioning business until 1850 when operations were finally ceased. During the Civil War, General Lee sent Confederate scouts to check on the forge. He wanted to make sure it was not being used to produce munitions for the North.

Codorus Furnace then entered a state of disrepair and neglect until 1949 when it was purchased by the Conservation Society of York County. The forge has been restored three times - most recently in 1983. It was listed on the National Registry of Historic Places in 1991.

The ghost stories related to Codorus Furnace are somewhat vague, but many have reported seeing that ubiquitous spectre of spook stories worldwide, the woman in white. The ghostly woman has been seen exiting the furnace house and walking the hills behind the forge. She is assumed to be the wife of one of the ironmasters, or perhaps a victim of the cruel manager.

A few of the ghost story books (almost as common as the women-in-white who haunt their pages) speak of a furnace master named Trego. This would have been Henry Trego, an ironmaster under Grubb or one of Grubb's descendants. It's difficult to find much information on this man, and it looks like most of the ghost books which report on Codorus Furnace use each other as references, but so the story goes: Trego was a cruel and strict manager. When his workers came for pay, Trego's wife would hand them their money from the window of the furnace house. Drunk or unruly workers would be imprisoned in the basement of the house. Some tales report that a human skull was found under the floorboards of the furnace house sometime in the 1980's.

Unprovable history and unconfirmed discovery of human remains aside, Codorus Furnace, like so many other forges, has an eerie, supernatural reputation. Perhaps it is the furnace that has summoned the Hidebehind, the hairy monsters, the ghosts, the black dogs, and all of the other spookiness associated with Toad Road - as that road led to, and around, the forge.

• • •

Codorus Furnace. 2016. [TR]

10
EXPLORING TOAD ROAD

There are many people who say they have walked Toad Road. In internet forums and comment sections many claim to have made it past the third, fourth, or even fifth gate, for instance. There is only one physical gate - at the corner where Trout Run Road and Range Road meet. There is a second farm gate, directly inside the first, to the right, which leads to a gas line right of way. As this gate technically leads one OFF of Toad Road, it can hardly be counted.

Dubious are any claims of other physical gates. They are not there. Slightly more believable are those who say that fallen trees across Toad Road *represent* gates. However, there are several such trees - far more than seven. So, which trees count as "gates"? It becomes a bit silly, trying to assign gates where there are none.

Other people claim that you must travel Toad Road at night to experience the Seven Gates. Taking this even further, others declare that it only works on *certain* nights - and the parameters vary from full moons, to Friday the thirteenth, to even *full moons on Friday the thirteenth only*. One could get a

On Toad Road. 2016. [TR]

headache trying to keep track of the hoops some people are willing to jump through in order to keep the Seven Gates legend at Toad Road. I have serious doubts that anyone has traveled the length of Toad Road at night, at least in recent times.

As Toad Road stands today, it can be a dicey hike even in broad daylight and good weather. It can be unclear where the trail heads at times. Walking Toad Road at night would become potentially treacherous. I do believe people have gone back Toad Road at night. I just doubt they got very far.

In May of 2016, I, along with two friends, walked the entirety of Toad Road - from the corner where Trout Run Road meets Ridge Road to the junction with Furnace Road, and then along River Farm Road until it rejoins with Furnace Road. In all, the trek adds up to about 3½ miles ranging from thick woods to open road. Some reports have Toad Road being as much as eight miles long. The closed section (between Trout Run Road and Furnace Road) is only a little over a mile.

Walking from the gate at Trout Run Road, each step is almost like stepping back in time. Each step feels like you are moving further from modern civilization and into a forgotten land. Nature has taken back the road. In places there is barely enough room for a man to get through, much less a car.

Over a fallen tree. Under another. Green grasses quickly give way to green leafy ground cover and the muddy trail leads on. White quartz speckles the ground in all directions. Branches crack underfoot and Toad Road shifts down, descending toward Codorus Creek.

Sounds of insects, birds, and running water fill the air. That watery sound grows louder - the creek and the streams that add to its flow, rushing toward the Susquehanna River,

Toad Road graffiti. '73 at the top. [TR]

make their power known. Approaching the fork where the Trout Run stream meets the Codorus, huge rocks, torn from the earth ages ago by some retreating glacier, can be seen on all sides. Where Toad Road crosses the Trout Run some of the rock faces show sections of deep green malachite. A bit further on, other rocks bear graffiti from long ago (" '73" reads one), but even this is now fading.

Toad Road follows the curving Codorus along its way. Rock juts high above the water on the opposite bank. Here it feels absolutely primordial. But for the few stray bottles, cans, tires, and other detritus of humanity - probably brought here and left in the woods by the Codorus when it flowed over its banks at various times - you may forget what year it is. Over the high hills there may be houses, but they might as well be in another country.

Red tail hawks scream above as if announcing the footfall of humans on this seldom-walked path. A white tail deer is stirred and bounds through the brush. There is a feeling here. There is a certain something in the air. The path continues along the creek before it turns again, up to meet Furnace Road.

To drive this road before it was closed must have been quite scenic. Gently descending into the hollow where the Trout Run meets Codorus Creek - then winding around with a view of the high rocks across the water. An old article about the area in a 1935 issue of *The White Rose Motorist* states "The view of the picturesque entrance of Trout Run into the creek will alone repay the traveler for his effort...".

It's easy to see why the township decided not to maintain Toad Road any longer. The creek must have washed out the road frequently. Hurricane Agnes must have been the final straw.

It is a shame Toad Road wasn't turned into a public hiking trail after the hurricane. Besides offering some beautiful views, this would have done much to dispel the outrageous stories of burning insane asylums and mad doctors.
As it stands, the questions linger: Why did they make it private? Were they afraid of something?

The answer to these questions may be very mundane. Perhaps the township lacked funding to maintain Toad Road as a trail. Perhaps they thought reverting it to private land would stop kids from going back there and doing what kids do.

But the stories of strange encounters on Toad Road persist. Those screams. The footfalls. That hairy monster.

Once on our hike there was movement of something large to my left. I looked, but I saw nothing. A few steps later one of my companions heard what he thought were voices from the same direction. We stopped to listen but heard nothing else out of the ordinary.

Where Trout Run meets Toad Road - the mystery figure is the dark spot on the left bank. [TR]

We lost the path once and had to backtrack to find our way. It would be easy to lose the path for good if you were not paying attention. It would be extremely difficult to stay on Toad Road at night.

I went looking through the many photos I had taken of Toad Road, trying to find anything unusual, spooky, or out of place. In one photo I did find something odd. It is most likely a tree stump, a rock, and a case of pareidolia (a natural human psychological phenomenon where the mind perceives a face or pattern in random groupings of objects). However, it looks strangely like a large dog head. The picture was taken where the Trout Run meets Toad Road.

A closeup of the mystery figure from the bank of Trout Run. [TR]

I almost decided not to include the photograph, as it is inconclusive at best and most likely a simple case of mistaken identity. My wife is a skeptic by nature. In this, she makes a great match for me - often providing simple and clear mundane explanations for images and videos I am looking at in my paranormal research. I showed her the photo from Toad Road, however, and asked her what she thought. Her response was something along the lines of, "That is *REALLY* creepy." I have included the original photo plus a closeup of the "dog head" figure. Is it a ghost? A rock? A spookwolf? A black dog? A stump? A dogman?

Flint mill ruins beside Codorus Creek. 2016. [AEH]

If we take the idea that Toad Road may have included, at one time, the entire length of T945, then we continue onto Furnace Road, still paralleling the Codorus. Looking toward the creek, there are ruins of an old flint mill, dating from the 1800's. Arched stone above the windows and doors show a care in construction and design we have lost to time.

The roof fell in long ago. Tiles of Delta slate lie broken and scattered about the area. Beams rot on the ground, splitting to reveal old iron nails, slowly rusting away. Antique farm equipment, last pulled across the field who-knows-when, sits now red-brown with rust among the ruins, tangled in weeds.

More than a decade ago, a local fellow told me this ruin was in some way related to the furnace (it technically dates from 1884, after the furnace ceased operation). It was the same man, having lived in the area since the 1970's, who showed me where Toad Road met Furnace Road. When I asked him about strange stories, ghosts, things in the woods, or the like, he simply pointed toward the furnace. He offered no other information.

Looking into the flint mill ruins along Codorus Creek. 2016. [TR]

When the Codorus is low here, the pollution is sadly evident. The banks are strewn with shoes, tires, bottles, cans, broken toys, and all manner of garbage. Presumably this has all been rushing here from York to settle along the way whenever the Codorus draws back from the banks. It is a heartbreaking sight to behold. The Codorus Creek also stinks. It has smelled terrible since the mid-1900's. I am told this stench has something to do with pollutants dumped in the creek by a paper company upstream. They have supposedly stopped dumping in the creek, but it still stinks. Throughout York County it is often called "the inky stinky Codorus". The combination of the unpleasant odor and the garbage can be both terribly sad and rather sickening. Deer and raccoon tracks cross the muddy banks to the water. I hate to think of the poor animals drinking that water.

Walking on, Codorus Furnace rises through the trees on a hill to the right. An impressive sight today, it must have been truly ominous in the days of its operation - spewing heat, smoke, fire, and molten iron. Perhaps the fiery furnace was the "Hell" into which Toad Road was supposed to lead? Perhaps in some subconscious way, or through some grain of folk-memory, the fires of Codorus Furnace, extinguished long ago, inspired stories of Hell. A winding, abandoned road - Toad Road - which led almost directly to those fires, could have become the local version of a "highway to hell".

Upon the hill, behind the furnace, are more ruins - little more than partial walls, which seem to be held up by climbing vines as much as crumbling masonry. Again, I heard something large moving in the brush beyond the ruined walls. I saw nothing.

Continuing along the creek and onto River Farm Road - past residences on both sides of the water. The road gets rougher and less inviting the further you travel. At a sharp right, away from the creek, River Farm Road begins a long ascent up a hill. There is a gate here, to close this section during the winter or when weather makes it impassible.

The gate on River Farm Road. [TR]

A small stream cuts a deep gully beside the road. More water making its way from the Hellam Hills to the rushing Codorus. Trees rise high on either side of the uphill climb.

Here, River Farm Road is barely more than a dirt road. If the closed section of Toad Road was in a similar state before Hurricane Agnes, it is easy to see how nature reclaimed so much and turned it into a mere path.

It's a long climb. Looking for any oddities - the telephone lines were cut in several places, and are left hanging from the poles. Not much else seems out of the ordinary, though if I were to talk about feelings and impressions, I think the mood on River Farm Road is more lonesome even than on Toad Road. This section particularly feels like a place we should not be, even though it is a public road.

Cut telephone lines hang along River Farm Road. [TR]

Eventually the woods clear a bit and fields open up the view. The hill is now a gentler grade. Then the trees close in again. There's not much to see but trees. To the left, a hunting blind sits perhaps 75 yards into the woods. To the right, more trees. On both sides, tree breaks.

I am far from an expert on bigfoot in general or tree breaks specifically. There are so many tree breaks throughout these woods, however, that I felt it pertinent to note them. Many researchers state that tree breaks, stick formations, and twisted branches are signs of the creatures' presence. Others say unless you *see* a creature making the breaks, it is not safe to assume it was the work of a bigfoot. It seems everywhere you look here trees are broken six, eight, ten feet off the ground,

River Farm Road. 2016. [AEH]

their trunks now downturned, branches touching the earth instead of reaching skyward.

    The woods are thin here, and not terribly deep. Certainly this is no place in which a large creature could live or hide. It makes no sense and it seems silly to even ponder. Unless they neither live nor hide here, but just pass through? From where? For what reasons? The Goblin Universe is laughing, somewhere.

    The road turns right again and heads back to meet Furnace Road. We've made a huge semi-circle around the furnace. We've walked Toad Road - or what might have been

Toad Road - from the gate at the corner of Trout Run Road to the end of River Farm Road. I have no hard evidence and no sightings of my own. I can only go on feelings and stories of other peoples' encounters.

I will be back.

One of many tree breaks along River Farm Road. [TR]

• • •

11
SO WHERE ARE THE SEVEN GATES OF HELL (AGAIN)?

Of course, as all good urban legends go, York County isn't the *ONLY* place to have Seven Gates of Hell. Several locales, including Chester County and Loretto in Pennsylvania, as well as others in Kansas, Texas, and Ohio have all laid claim to hosting The Seven Gates of Hell.

Why *SEVEN* gates? Perhaps it's just old lucky number seven rearing it's head again - seven dwarves, seven yellow gypsies, the seventh son of a seventh son, seven deadly sins, etc. In fact one of the other towns which hosts the Seven Gates of Hell claims that each of the seven deadly sins is experienced as one passes through the consecutive gates.

In fairy tales and folklore you will find sevens everywhere. Dante's Hell had *NINE* circles, though, so why *SEVEN* gates? Again, the answer has likely been lost to time and whispering down the lane, but I will make a guess: In the mid-20th century a popular lecture among evangelist preachers was "The Seven Gates to Hell". Catchy, isn't it? I think it was very catchy among those with an interest in the supernatural and superstitions and general spookiness, and it made the leap from being a concept to referring to actual geographical places.

Because there probably never were seven physical gates at any of these places in York County (and definitely not on Toad Road), it's hard to pin them down to any one place. So, if someone comes along and publishes a book with broad circulation (like *Weird USA* et al.), and they claim finally to have located the Seven Gates in York County, once and for all - then many readers will think that they've done the hard work, and it's in print, so it must be true.

The Seven Gates of Hell are nowhere - but they may yet exist. How is that for a koan? Here is where we leap from history and maps into the realms of the purely paranormal. As part of the collective folk memory of generations in York County, perhaps all of this concentration on and searching for the Seven Gates have made them into a kind of tulpa or egregore: thought forms made real. Seven markers of the unknown - gateways into the dangerous *OTHER*. Portals into the Goblin Universe. Psychic mile markers on Toad Road, itself a gateway to Codorus Furnace, and on over the Susquehanna River to Chickies Rock where the albatwitches play their flutes with such beautiful music that people are lured away and never return.

So let's go onward. Let's go beyond. Beyond the Seventh Gate and on to other true reports of strange things in York, Adams, and Lancaster counties...

• • •

12
THE ALBATWITCHES AND CHICKIES ROCK

Chickies Rock County Park is located between Marietta and Columbia, right along the Susquehanna River in Lancaster County. It is described in *Pennsylvania Fireside Tales, volume III*, as "one of the most haunted sections in the entire state". Standing on the Lancaster side of the river, you can gaze west and easily see the Hellam Hills on the York County side. It is precisely at this place, looking across the river, that I began to see the close geographical relationship which exists between many of the places which I am writing about in this volume. The Codorus Creek empties into the Susquehanna a little bit north, around a bend in the river - but as the crow flies, it is not far at all. What are the chances the very strange but very similar occurrences happening in both places are not somehow related? Of course, this would be as difficult to prove as the phenomena themselves - but it would seem to be ignoring a potential piece to the puzzle if geographic proximity were not noted. Also of note, there was at one time eight iron furnaces located between Marietta and Columbia. *SEVEN* of these forges were located within the bounds of Chickies Rock.

Among the many strange tales associated with the Chickies Rock area are all manner of ghost stories, glowing

Ruins of a Furnace at Chickies Rock. 2016. [TR]

lights, orbs, screams from the woods and, once again, bigfoot encounters. Strange mists are seen drifting through the trees at Chickies Rock; treetops move with no sign of wind; the sound of drumming is heard, yet no drummers are ever found. Shadow People, dark featureless entities which many people feel are negative or demonic in nature, have also been seen running through the park. Unfortunately, Chickies Rock has also been the site of many falls and suicides over the years - only adding to its dark reputation.

The ghostly tales surrounding Chickies Rock are said to date back to well before the Europeans settled into Columbia and Marietta.

Ruins associated with another furnace at Chickies Rock. 2016. [AEH]

There was said to have been a great battle, 100 years before William Penn's time, over disputed land between Chiques Creek and Little Chiques Creek. The warriors on each side were said to number over 600 strong. After two days' battle, only twelve survived. A prophet declared the spirits of the fallen warriors would not enter into the afterlife until the land was shared by the twelve survivors of the battle.

A slightly more recent tale involves a Romeo and Juliet-like tragedy involving a white man and a Native American woman. In some stories she is a maiden while in others she is married. She would meet her white Romeo atop Chickies Rock. The story varies - but the tragedy is the same - her love interest dies fighting for her and she either jumps from Chickies Rock in despair - or is thrown by her jealous husband. Her death is the result in all versions of the story. Some say the area is haunted by the spirits of the ill-fated lovers.

Chickies Rock - looking toward Marietta. Image from an old postcard.

A much more horrifying apparition greeted Harriet Horn in 1946 when picnicking with co-workers at Chickies Hill. Harriet and an unnamed man drove off to retrieve some water. Before their car left the park, they came upon a terrible creature. 16-feet high, and very thin. The being either had no arms and legs or they were obscured by the trees - it is difficult to tell from Harriet's description. However, she did recall strange details about the creature: the giant was wrapped like a mummy with three knives protruding from each side of its horrid head.

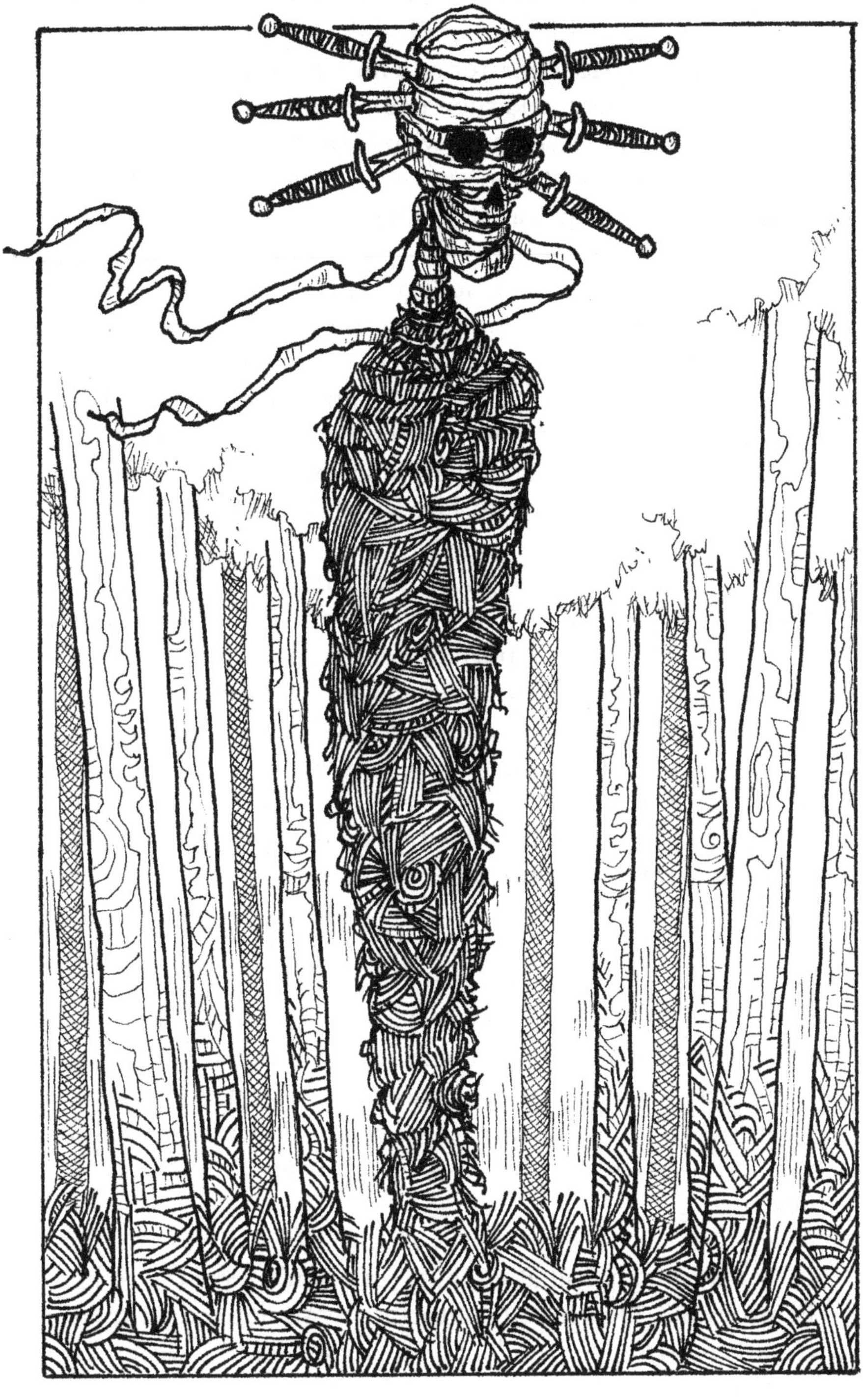

Harriet's companion saw it as well. Exclaiming, "My God, what is it?!," he was barely able to drive the vehicle. They pulled off the road a quarter of a mile from the park, in disbelief and shock, and then realized their co-workers were still at the picnic. Returning with great speed, they told their co-workers "You gotta get out of here, we saw something terrible!" The picnic was abandoned.

It is unclear if Harriet's other co-workers saw the creature, but they must have seen something, for the next day at work everyone was quiet except one old woman. This woman told a tale of a witch that had lived on Chickies Hill. The witch was said to have been evicted from her home, at which time she placed a curse on the area that lingers today. Yet another witch, so close to Marietta where The River Witch made her home!

In 1969 a kind of ghost mania infected the area, with hundreds of curious onlookers coming to Chickies Park at night after some teenagers reported seeing a ghost there. Though the teenagers later said they made up their sighting, one apparition was seen by hundreds of ghost-seekers. They said it was a silver-grey mist moving through the woods well above ground level. At least one of the onlookers got a better look at the form. He said its head appeared to be wrapped in bandages, with a knife sticking from the wrappings.

There are much smaller, and far older creatures that seem to have been associated with the Chickies Rock area as long as anyone can remember. The albatwitches. These four-to-five foot tall, skinny, hair-covered ape-men seem to be much more than juvenile bigfoot, as some have suggested. Known for their love of apples, albatwitches were said to be hunted to extinction in the 1800's. However, sightings continue to this day.

The name, albatwitch, is commonly reported to be a Pennsylvania Dutchified compound word derived ultimately from English 'applesnitch', i.e. 'apple-stealer'. However, *alb* is a

German word for an 'elf' or spirit. Given the nature of the creatures, it seems at least as likely that albatwitch might be a mixed compound word, combining German 'alb' + English 'witch', i.e. 'elf-witch' or 'spirit-witch'. Another possibility is that the word is derived from a combination of German 'alb' with Pennsylvania Dutch *snitz* - 'snitz' being a Pennsylvania Dutch term for apples. This would give the word the sense of 'apple-elf' or 'apple-spirit'.

The Susquehannock Indians knew well of the albatwitch, and painted images of the creatures on their war shields. The Algonquin also told of small hairy hominid creatures known as Megumoowesoos. Like the Celtic fairies, Megumoowesoos were said to lure people into the woods with wonderful music. Bewitched by the sound of the creatures' flutes, many who heard and followed the flute songs disappeared. Here again we have the recurring idea of a creature (or other phenomenon) either luring people into the woods, or else taking people already in the woods, with the people in either case never being seen again.

The albatwitches were said to live mostly in the trees. Preferring to keep to the shadows, they made their presence known by a sound like a cracking whip (perhaps this is aggressive branch-breaking, a well known bigfoot trait?). Picnickers at Chickies Rock have reported their apples stolen and sometimes even thrown back at them.

Local paranormal researcher and author Rick Fisher saw an albatwitch himself one morning before sunrise in February 2002. Driving toward Marietta on Route 23, Fisher saw what he first assumed to be a human walking in the middle of the road. As he got closer, he realized it was no human at all, but a five foot tall, very skinny biped, covered with hair. When he slowed his vehicle and turned on the high beams to get a better look, the creature turned around showing its two yellow eyes ... and then vanished from sight.

In Fisher's book *Ghosts of the River Towns,* he has collected another albatwitch report from the area as well. In 2002, about two miles from his own sighting, a group of friends were driving on Pinkerton Road when a thin, hair-covered, bipedal creature crossed the road in front of them.

A more recent albatwitch sighting comes from the other side of the river, near Red Lion, York County. The website *Phantoms and Monsters* reports that on July 18, 2008, a woman was driving about two miles outside of Red Lion on Route 624. She noticed something running across a field. Pulling over to observe the oddity, she saw a four foot tall bipedal creature, covered in sparse dark grey hair. The witness said the head of the cryptid was smaller than that of a human child of the same height. She watched the creature for several minutes, saying it would stop, look around, and then continue running again, until it finally reached a patch of woods.

• • •

13
ERD LICHTES, SPOOKLIGHTS, AND UFOS

The Pennsylvania Dutch had a name for the strange drifting lights that so many people report in conjunction with mysterious places - *erd lichtes* or "earth lights". Sometimes called "jack-o'-lanterns", "ghost lights", or by the more familiar name, "will-o'-the-wisps", these uncanny lights have been seen in Pennsylvania as long as anyone can remember. In recent times, erd lichtes are generally referred to as "orbs" - and they may or may not be related to the orb phenomenon that often shows up in photographs of places said to be haunted.

These flickering, eerie lights became a part of "weird" Pennsylvania folklore long before the invention of photography. People were warned never to follow the lights. Seemingly guided by some form of intelligence, the glowing globes would lead people through the trees, until they became lost - and sometimes lost forever.

It is said you should not chase the will-o'-the-wisps. They cannot be caught - always dancing ahead or flickering out like a blown candle when one gets too close. If the lights did not lead you into oblivion, there was the chance that when you gave up the chase, the lights would turn and follow you instead. When the Europeans arrived in Pennsylvania, they were warned

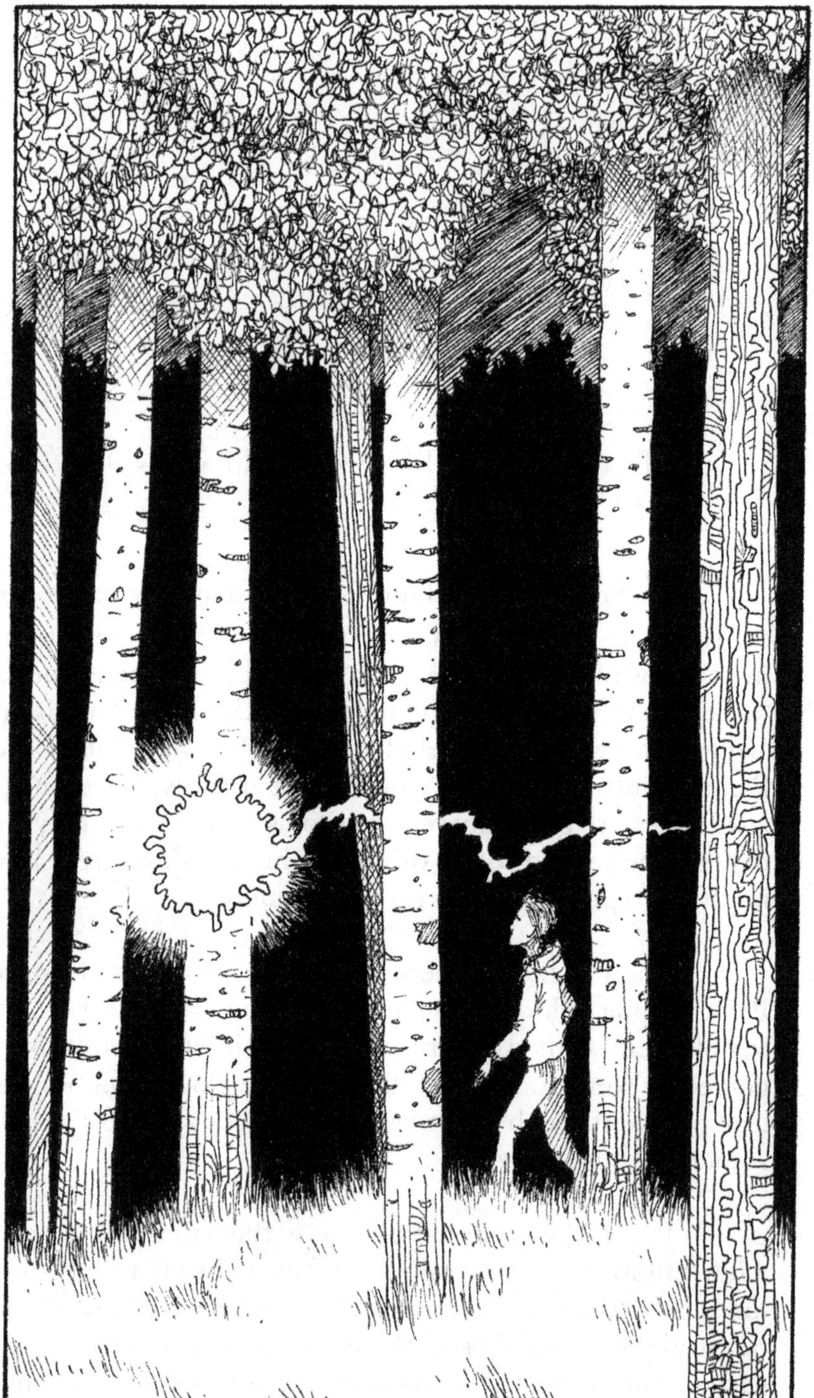

by the Nanticoke that the ominous lights would pursue people, and bring them misfortune.

Ghost lights have been associated with Hex Hollow, Toad Road, and Chickies Rock. Strange lights sometimes accompany bigfoot sightings as well - which have been reported at all of these places. Who can say what it means? The coincidences abound.

UFOs, too, have been seen throughout the area. So many ghost story books have been written about Gettysburg that it's easy to forget that other strange things have happened in the town. On July 4, 1947 - 84 years and one day after the Battle of Gettysburg that left so many of its dead to haunt the fields and town here - no less than sixteen witnesses reported seeing strange grey, shiny discs flying over the battlefield. The objects were flying in formation, rolling as they flew. The witnesses estimated the objects were flying 150-200 feet above the ground but were only about six inches in diameter. Small objects, but still unidentified and flying.

On February 20, 1973, one woman saw an object which she said "horrified" her in the skies west of Stewartstown. She said the object was just hovering in the sky and about three times the size of the full moon as it appears on the horizon. It was a mottled dark red in color, and elongated. She was sure it wasn't the Northern Lights or a weather balloon.

October of 1973 was particularly active for strange lights in the sky. Newspaper accounts tell of UFO sightings over various places in York County - Yoe, Yorkana, Windsor, Locust Grove, Felton, and Mt. Wolf all reported UFOs the same night, October 14. Even police officers reported sightings. In Felton, where there were three UFOs in the sky at once, witnesses said they could see a red beam shining down from the objects toward the ground - and white beams being shot from UFO to UFO in the sky.

The following night sightings continued - near the Susquehanna River in Delta, less than a mile from Peach Bottom Atomic power plant, a red and blue object with rotating lights was observed in the sky by several people. While in Shiloh-Weigelstown, a man who described himself as a skeptic saw a bright orange light in the sky and admitted, "This was something out of the ordinary."

October 20, 1973 brought the orange glow back to the skies in the area; this time to East Berlin, Adams County. Jackson Township Police Chief Lloyd Adams and nine other people witnessed a "blimp-like" object with an orange glow at the front and multi-colored lights at the tail end. October 22 saw a greenish-blue disk shaped object over Hanover, reported by an amateur astronomer who was certain it wasn't a star or planet.

UFO sightings in the area continued through the 1970's, but not with the same intensity and geographical concentration of sightings as those in October 1973. 1977 brought some incidents which may indicate UFOs landing in local fields.

On March 8, 1977, eleven witnesses in multiple locations observed a red ball of light moving against the wind in Gatchellville, York County. The ball of light was observed wobbling through the sky for 25 minutes. The ball dropped to earth and started a grass fire in a field. The fire burned an area of 30 by 100 feet. Within the burnt field was an unburnt area in the shape of a triangle. At the point of each triangle was a hole in the ground. The area was tested and radioactivity was detected. The soil was burnt black to a depth of three inches, suggesting the fire burned with intense heat.

Something strange happened in a cornfield south of Loganville, York County in October or November of 1977. A hunter noticed a section of broken and burned cornstalks in a field - 25 feet wide and 40 feet long burnt, broken, and bent toward the east. No one could say what had caused the damage

- no evidence was found that it was the work of human vandals or a prank. UFOs were speculated as the cause.

In 1978 York County was experiencing a wave of strange events. UFOs were reported over the York County Shopping Center. Meanwhile, in the southeastern section of the county, Muddy Creek, Fawn Grove, Delta, and Peach Bottom residents were reporting both UFO and bigfoot sightings.

On a property near Fawn Grove, Robert Brown reported a bright reddish object landed in a field. Whatever it was, it caused a fire in the shape of a circle and firemen had to be called to extinguish the blaze. A military helicopter was seen observing the landing site the following day. (This report sounds very similar to the Gatchellville landing above. Gatchellville is near Fawn Grove. Either two very similar incidents happened within a year around the same area, or this event has been reported as happening in both 1977 and 1978.)

Turning the clock forward to January 20, 1995, a witness from Dallastown, York County reports a strange night of lights in the skies. The witness and several friends observed a series of lights slowly hovering over the hills and horizons outside of town. The lights moved again and again in the same pattern. After watching the lights repeat the same cycle for over a half hour, three low-flying military-type helicopters flew overhead toward the mystery lights. After watching the lights for over an hour the pattern changed. A pulsing red light connected with one of the other lights. Firework-like sparks were emitted and the object flashed bright in the sky. The flash was bright enough to cause several of the observers to turn away. One of the observers even fell backward.

A hexagonal or octagonal shaped craft was seen above Red Lion, York County, on March 9, 2009. The witnesses included a mother and two daughters who observed a white, "almost blinding", light in the sky. As the object approached at a low altitude, the witness described its size as being larger than a

747 airplane. They noticed that is was a series of white lights around the edges of the hexagonal/octagonal craft, not a single white light, which made the object so bright. They observed the UFO for about 5 minutes. It flew slowly overhead, turned, and flew off into the distance.

Spring Grove, York County, had UFOs in the sky in December 2009 and January 2010. At 5:45 am on December 27, 2009, a witness observed a slow, low flying light hovering above the trees. The object made a low humming sound and had three prongs protruding from the bottom. Each prong was lit with various colored lights. The same witness observed a beam of bright white light flash across the sky on January 11, 2010.

In 2011, strange crafts were seen above the Gettysburg Farms campground in Dover, York County, on several nights in one week. The observer, who submitted his report to MUFON (the Mutual UFO Network) and *Phantoms and Monsters*, saw the UFOs between August 15 and August 22, 2011. The man described the crafts as possibly triangle shaped and dark in color. Fire was emitted from the bottom of the crafts, like a rocket's exhaust flames. The crafts passed slowly over the campground at a low altitude, but made no sound. Each time he saw the UFOs, they seemed to materialize in the sky to the east, without making a sound.

The first observation was on August 15 at about 8:40 pm. The craft was followed by a second, similar unknown object which followed the same path as the first. Both crafts seemed to just disappear into the sky as they passed into the distance. The second observation was on August 17 at about 8:45 pm. Two crafts were again observed, starting in the east and disappearing into the night sky - though the crafts followed a different course of travel on this evening. The third sighting occurred on August 18 at 8:45 pm. Only one craft was observed, however it followed the same flight path and disappeared as the others had on previous evenings. On August 20, the witness observed the craft again, at about 8:30 pm. On this evening the craft again followed the same pattern but this time it was followed by two similar objects. All of the UFOs followed the same flight path and disappeared as they had on the previous evenings.

2013 saw UFOs again appearing over the area. First, in Lancaster County, triangular craft were reported flying low over Adamstown. The brief report on the UFO Research Center of Pennsylvania website notes that there was some sort of telepathic contact and a possible abduction associated with the sightings. There is no date given, but the report was posted on the website on March 13, 2013.

On March 14, 2013, a man in Wrightsville, York County, observed what he described as a huge circle of lights early in the morning. He described a perfect circle of bright white lights about the size of a jet airplane. On the right and left sides of the object, pulsating sets of lights changed colors. He observed the object fly across the Susquehanna River and into the skies above Lancaster County.

In June of 2013 the UFO Research Center of Pennsylvania reported another sighting above York County. The site notes multiple witness reports of a bright sphere moving from South to East in the sky. The object made no sound and moved with "fluidity".

Seven Valleys has long been host to strange spooklights. In 2006, local York musician Don Belch traveled to Seven Valleys regularly for band practice at a friend's house. Above a field, just off Walters Hatchery road, he and his bandmates noticed an eerie green glow in the sky. They watched the weird light hover for a time but then it suddenly descended with great speed into the field. As time passed, they had mostly forgotten the encounter until the owners of the house where they practiced mentioned that they liked living there very much - except sometimes there was a strange green light that shined through their windows and disturbed them at night.

Another local musician, Angel Mercado, was dating a woman who lived in Seven Valleys around the same time. Angel saw the green lights on more than one occasion. Like strange green flashes of lightning, the lights would shine through the windows, illuminating dark rooms. Angel's girlfriend had been raised in Seven Valleys. She and her family had all seen the lights in the past. No one knew what they were.

Lynne Strayer, besides being a long-time resident of Seven Valleys, is a bit of an amateur historian and a collector of strange tales of local origin. She told me her father saw a yellowish glow in a field on his Seven Valleys property one night in 1981. He could not figure out the cause of the glow.

I have seen, myself, unexplained lights in York County. In September 2012 on Mt. Olivet Road, heading north - just past Rehmeyer's Hollow Road about where Shangrila Road meets Mt. Olivet Road - I was a passenger in a car driving at about 3:30 am. To the northeast an area of the hills and trees were lit up as bright as day - not by a green light, but by a blue-white glow. I could not determine the source of the light - nor even the direction from which the light was shining. A large area of the fields and trees was illuminated by an unnatural glow. The driver of the vehicle was tired and in no shape to pursue unexplained lights, so I could do no more than wonder at the phenomenon and stare as we passed. I make a point to look for these lights each time I am driving Mt. Olivet Road in darkness. I have never seen them since.

My sighting may not be unique. In the 1890's *The York Daily* featured occasional reports from the Rehmeyer's Hollow area entitled *Rehmeyer's Valley Jottings*. On July 21 of 1892 the column questioned, "Did you see the northern lights Saturday last, and can you tell us what caused them?" Perhaps the author was talking about the actual Northern Lights, though it is quite rare to see them this far south - but perhaps it was the same lights that I witnessed, to the north of the Hollow, 120 years later.

Whether these lights are crafts piloted by beings from other dimensions, different manifestations of will-o'-the-wisps, or something else entirely, we may never know. Nevertheless, where you have other paranormal phenomena, unusual lights seem to occur as well.

• • •

14
BIGFOOT CREATURES

Bigfoot creatures are perhaps the most commonly encountered cryptids both in south central Pennsylvania and in the United States in general. Before "Bigfoot" and "Sasquatch" became common terms, people were encountering wild men of the woods. In medieval England they were called wodewose and most American Indian tribes had more than one name for the creatures (in fact, many tribes would identify more than one type of hairy hominid). In old newspapers, they were often referred to as "giants", "wild-men", or "hairy men,"; after the 'discovery' of the mountain gorilla, they were sometimes called gorillas.

In our area, sightings probably went back to the times the first humans walked through the woods here, long before the Europeans arrived - but stories of wild-men have been appearing in our local newspapers for well over a century and a half.

In December of 1858 multiple witnesses in Lancaster reported seeing a wild-man. They described him as having the shape of a man, but being covered with hair, like a bear. A farmer caught the creature suckling his cows. It fled, leaping away as easily as a deer. In August of 1871 a "hairy man" is reported again in Lancaster. The creature was accused of "afflicting children and livestock".

A wild-man was reported in the Bottstown area of York on December 6, 1872. This creature was reported as a "spook" in the shape of a wild-man. The article states that the creature caused great excitement among the residents.

In September of 1874, *The Reading Times* published an article stating that "every year about this time...a wild-man of immense stature and terrible aspect" made its appearance in the area of Morgantown (Lancaster/Berks/Chester Counties). Witnesses described the creature as having an "altogether horrible appearance". It was nearly seven feet tall, with hands and feet double the size of those of an average man. The creature was said to exclaim in "unearthly yells" and "demonaic laughs" as he carried stolen sheep and pigs off to the forest. The locals tried to hunt the creature down, with no success. Each time the brave hunters encountered the wild-man, it gave a scream and leapt away before anyone could pull the trigger. In the words of one witness, "It is simply terrible and of ferocious aspect."

Hanover, in York County, had its own hairy "spook" prowling the streets in March of 1883. The creature was described as having the "dual form" of a man and a bear. This "hideous looking affair" was seen many nights - usually from the hours of 11:00 pm to midnight. Several people were chased by the creature, which they described as "most terrifying". The newspaper article noted that many bachelors had stopped calling on young women, or cut their visits short, for fear of running into the creature at night.

One night in late October of 1886, Mr. and Mrs. Nehemiah Cooper and some friends were returning from evening church services at Mt. Nebo Church in Delta, York County. They encountered a "monster" twelve-to-fifteen feet

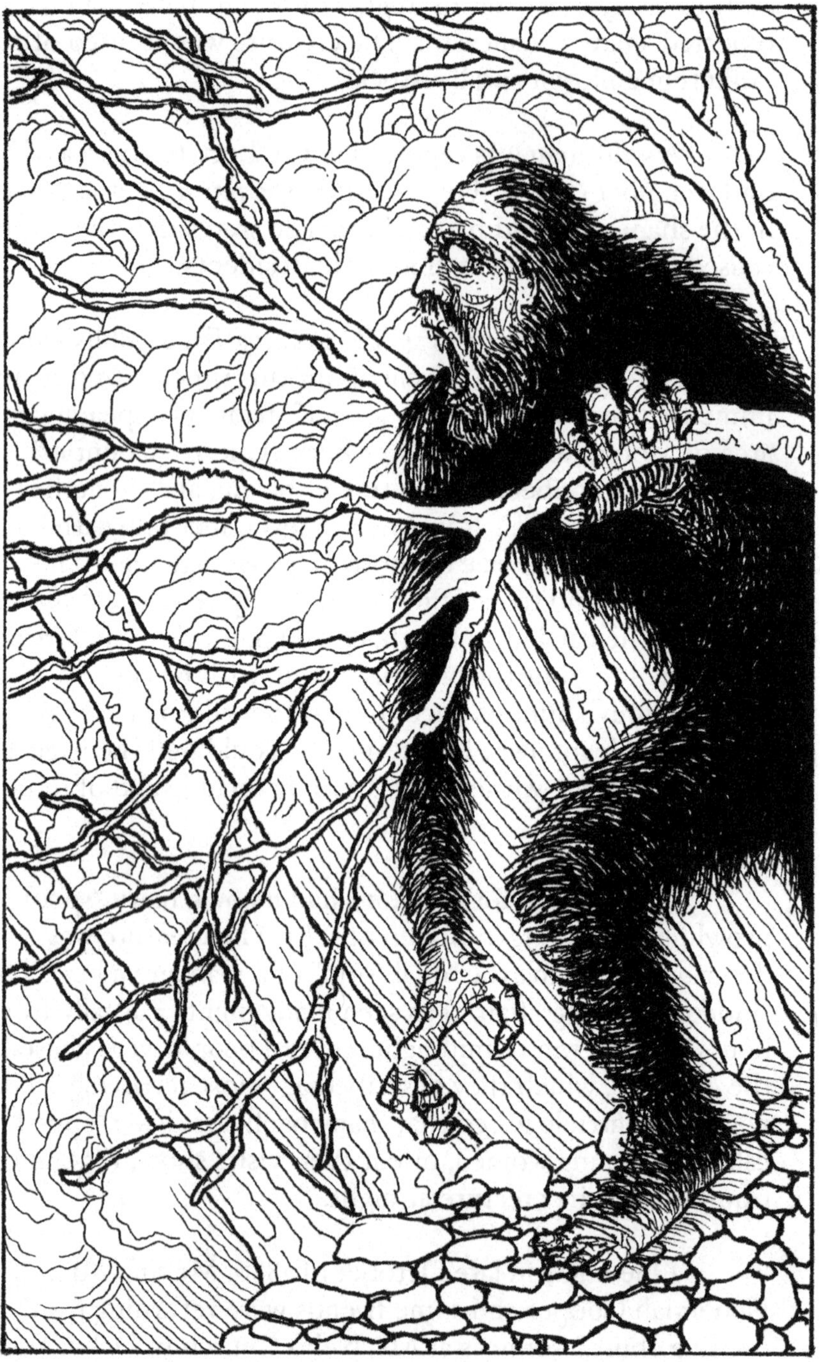

tall and six feet across at the shoulders. They began to throw rocks at the creature, believing it at first to be some kind of prank. However, when the creature started advancing toward them they turned and fled.

In 1902 mountain gorillas were "discovered" in Africa - or more accurately, encountered by Europeans for the first time. This large great ape captured the imagination of the public, and gave newspapers a new name to hang on bigfoot creatures. 1921 was an exciting year as what would become known as the Gettysburg Gorilla made its appearance in Adams and surrounding counties. It is likely that this was more than one creature, but because seeing these creatures is such an unusual event, reports of any hairy bipeds were thought to refer to the same creature.

In northern Adams County, a frightening "gorilla" was causing surprise and concern among residents. Little credence was given to initial witnesses until the number of reports greatly increased. The creature prowled about the vicinity and helped itself to the contents of at least one smokehouse.

On January 20, 1921, residents of Idaville, Adams County, chased a "huge gorilla" throughout the afternoon and evening. It was first seen between York Springs and Idaville where some men attempted to capture or shoot the creature. They were unsuccessful, but by 10:00 that night 50 men gathered near Idaville and attempted to hunt down the "gorilla". The creature again escaped across the hills.

On January 25, a poor mule was the victim, not of the "gorilla", but of mistaken identity. Abraham Lau of Franklintown, York County, having heard the stories of the wandering "gorilla" mistook his neighbor's mule for the creature. Lau grabbed his gun, shot, and injured the mule.

"Gorilla" sightings continued in the area - not confined to Adams County, but ranging across Franklin County and into

Frederick County, Maryland. On January 26, in Rouzerville, Franklin County, the creature was seen in an alley. A gun toting mob formed and chased the creature into the mountains. Another innocent victim was shot. This time a dog was killed as an excited hunter fired, mistaking it for the "gorilla." While the hunters searched the woods, the creature returned to the town, causing great panic. It was next seen near the Moneterey golf course, crawling on all fours. When men called at the creature it rose on two legs and approached them "making gurgling sounds". In late January the creature was seen again in Pen Mar, Franklin County. The witness saw the "gorilla" in broad daylight walking through a field.

Some months later, the Gettysburg Gorilla appeared on York Street in Gettysburg itself. In early August, a woman saw the creature moving along the fence behind her house. In fear, she ran to her neighbor, who in turn grabbed his shotgun. He fired at the creature which dropped to the ground. As the man approached, the beast jumped up and chased him back into the house. The "gorilla" departed in the direction of Biglerville. Footprints of the creature were then discovered in a nearby field. Sightings were also reported in York Springs and Gardners, Adams County.

After ranging across the mountains and into neighboring counties, the "gorilla" made its last noted appearance of 1921 in Adams County on August 21. Ray Weikert was riding his horse along Fairfield Road when a five foot tall bipedal creature walked leisurely across the road in front of him, climbed a fence, and disappeared into the brush. Weikert's horse nearly bolted at the sight of the hairy biped.

In 1957 a bigfoot was spotted south of Hanover in York County. Helena Weaver was parked in a wooded area when the creature approached her car with outstretched arms. She said the bigfoot was "very, very tall" - over seven feet. It had large eyes and was covered all over with brown hair. She thought the creature looked very old. Weaver said the creature was known to residents and had been seen by others in the area.

July 1, 1961 brought another sighting of a five foot tall hairy bipedal creature in Adams County. In the town of Greenmount, near Marsh Creek, a teenager encountered the creature. It was covered with long hair and emitted a foul odor - a feature commonly attributed to bigfoot.

A man was jogging the back roads of Tolna, York County, at night in 1965 when a "hairy thing" stepped out into the road in front of him. The bipedal creature looked at the jogger, then proceeded across the road.

In 1966 and 1967 there were sightings of a tall "gorilla" outside of Glen Rock, PA near Friendship Elementary School. At least one steer was found dead and "mangled" and other livestock deaths were blamed on the creature.

Sometime in the 1970's, a woman living alone in Felton, York County found footprints six feet apart. She also reported her dogs would issue a "horrible" bark at times, and an incident of an unexplained pounding on her roof.

In 1972, ecology teacher Bob Chance had an encounter with a possible bigfoot near Muddy Creek in York County. He was hiking along Muddy Creek with some students when they had several boulders thrown in their direction. Chance, at first, thought it was a landslide - but the projectiles followed his party as they made their way out of the area.

The creatures must have stayed around, for the Bigfoot Field Researchers Organization (BFRO) reports multiple encounters in the area of Peach Bottom / Delta between the years of 1973-1976. The reports state that a hair-covered man-like creature almost seven feet tall was seen repeatedly in the wooded sections and abandoned slate quarries around this area.

The encounters seemed to happen most frequently at the start and end of deer hunting season.

A truck driver from York hit a bigfoot creature on April 24, 1975, just south of Fawn Grove in Maryland. The creature ran from the road after impact, holding its chest and thigh, but it left some evidence behind. Police found flesh and long hair imbedded in the car. Bob Chance sent the hair samples to scientists in Seattle for analysis. The scientists determined the hair to be from a rare primate.

A family in Delta reported several incidents in 1975. A creature would issue cries so loud they seemed at times as if they were amplified. The cries would sometimes wake the mother up at night. The sounds were reported as howls from a distance which turned to growls as the creature approached. There were also incidents of the creature picking up and moving their garbage cans and coming onto the back porch of the house. The family was so disturbed by the repeated incidents that they felt the creature was "haunting" them.

As noted in the previous chapter, 1978 was a very weird year for York County. UFOs were seen over the county - including in the Delta/Fawn Grove/Muddy Creek area. Coinciding with the unidentified lights were bigfoot sightings.

On January 10, 1978, at about 10:00 pm, a witness saw a ten foot tall bigfoot creature in the woods near Kennard-Dale High School. As he watched the creature walk away, it turned its head to look back, showing shining white eyes. The witness also noticed a strong foul odor.

Before the end of the month, Allen Hilsmeier and his sons would find evidence that a bigfoot creature had trodden across his farm in Delta, York County. On the night of January 27, 1978, the Hilsmeier family dogs were unusually aggravated. They were barking loudly and running back and forth from the fields behind their house. Something back there had the two

German shepherds very upset. The following day, the Hilsmeiers found over two thousand footprints continuing for miles in the ice and snow on their farm, through the woods, over a barbed wire fence, across a creek, and over a distant hill. Each footprint was sixteen inches in length and six inches in width - with a depth indicating considerable weight. The creature's long stride left about five feet between successive tracks, which were placed one in front of the other, not staggered like human tracks. The creature maintained this five foot stride even up sharp inclines. Another strange feature, although one also occurring in other reports of bigfoot creatures in Pennsylvania, was: each print showed three large toes. This tri-toed track has been reported extensively by researcher Stan Gordon in bigfoot prints found on the western side of the state.

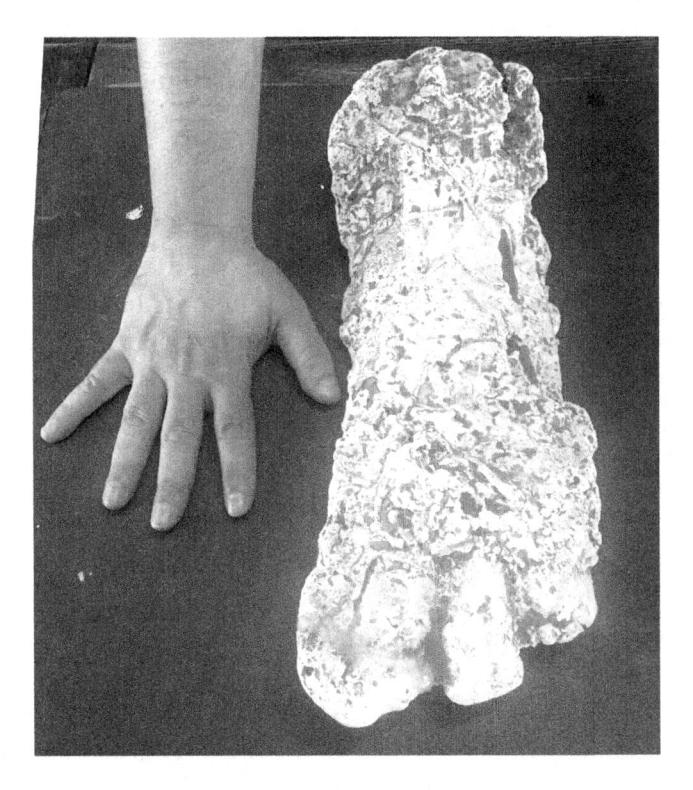

Three-toed bigfoot cast from the collection of Bob Chance. The author's hand shown for size comparison. Photo by Matt Jackson.

Hilsmeier called the Pennsylvania Game Commission to report the tracks. Without ever viewing the prints they said they were most likely deer tracks. Hilsmeier then called the closest newspaper, which happened to be the *Aegis* out of Bel Air, Maryland.

Two reporters came to his farm and, with Hilsmeier, again followed the prints. Eventually they came upon the remains of a rabbit - a bit of fur, blood, and a leg. Where the creature had crossed a fence, they found long, matted hair. Bigfoot researcher Bob Chance was then called to check out the scene. After following the tracks with Hilsmeier's sons, he found more hair samples and discovered that one set of footprints lead to a dead calf. The calf was determined to have died of natural causes, but something had been eating at the remains.

Allen Hilsmeier's son Jeff invited me to the farm one day in July of 2016. I met with Allen, Jeff, and the rest of the family, and we discussed the events of January 1978. They remembered it well, and provided many details which were not in the newspaper articles from the time. I was able to see just where the tracks were found, as well as see some of the hair samples they had collected. When I asked them if they had ever heard anything strange around the time of the sightings, Allen's wife Margaret told me a very interesting story. Late one evening in the summer of that year, she heard through and open window of their house some very loud howls coming from the direction of Muddy Creek. She said whatever made the sound must have had an immense lung capacity as, besides the volume, the sustain of the howl was very long. She described the tone as low and rather frightening - akin to the growling howls of the giant film gorilla Mighty Joe Young.

About a month after the tracks were found on the Hilsmeier farm, a driver headed toward Peach Bottom Atomic Power Station witnessed a tall creature dash across the road. Norval Thomas was driving a fuel oil truck down a long hill

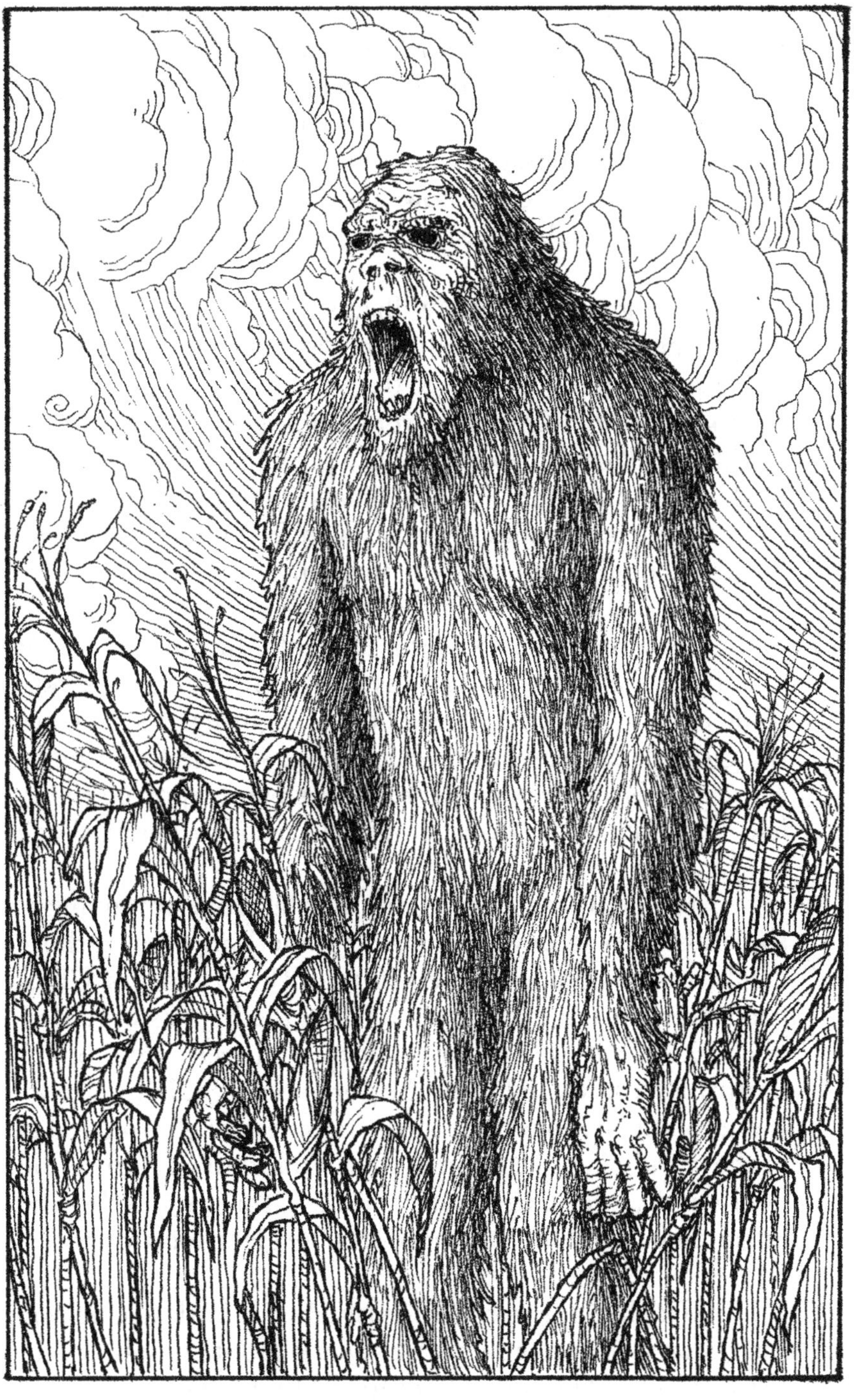

headed toward the power plant when he noticed what he thought was a huge man cross in front of him. As he passed the figure he noted it was over seven feet tall. He thought it was the biggest man he had ever seen - but then he realized that there shouldn't be any humans wandering around there at night. When he pulled into the power station Thomas told a security guard what he had witnessed.

The guard, Urlo C. Williams, along with Thomas and some other employees, took some flashlights and went to investigate. They found huge tracks - twice as big as a man's size 10½ boot print. While they were looking at the tracks they heard a shrill cry. It sounded like a pig, "but it wasn't a pig. It made your skin crawl," said Williams. The sound came from close to where Thomas saw the seven foot tall biped. They heard the chilling squeal two more times.

Another security guard, Donald Johnson, lived about a mile from the plant. He said his dogs were "going berserk" for some reason on the night of Thomas' sighting. A search around the grounds of the plant revealed more strange footprints. More guards at the plant came forward and reported they too had heard the eerie shrieks, four days prior to Thomas' sighting.

On February 13, 1978, another farm about ten miles from the Hillsmeier farm was attacked. Something opened the chicken coop door and killed all 30 of the occupants. Chicken heads were bitten off, twisted off, and the breasts were ripped open. Blood was sucked from the birds. Large three-toed footprints lead to and from the gory scene. Still other reports came rolling in around the area - sightings of glowing red eyes in the woods; spooked horses that refused to go into certain fields; lifeless dogs, their necks broken, thrown into high trees; lingering bad smells; and those strange giant footprints.

The bigfoot were not finished with York County. In early March of 1978 a motorist saw a bigfoot creature near Spring Grove. The police later found footprints in the snow.

Then in September, at 2:00 am one morning, something struck the side of a camper in Gifford Pinchot State Park. The blow was delivered with such force that the entire camper was shaken. The occupants looked outside the camper and saw a large shadow, cast by a creature that was backlit by some lights at the campground. A few minutes later the creature moved alongside the camper, turning the door handle as is it walked. A short time after that, the occupants heard a loud scream - which they described as sounding like a combination of a woman's scream and a siren - coming from the direction in which the creature walked. The occupants noticed a family staying nearby leave quickly after the incident.

Finishing out the year, in late November a hunter encountered a bigfoot creature near Holtwood Dam. After initially hearing the large creature, the hunter began to notice that it was pacing him in the woods. When he would walk, the creature would walk. When he stopped, it stopped. He stopped for about three minutes to listen. After the sound of gunshots came from another direction, the hunter heard loud crashing through the brush. The hunter caught a glimpse of the creature as it veered to the left of his position and moved out of sight, faster than any man. It was seven feet tall, and definitely not human. The hunter later returned to the scene and found large tracks.

Moving over to Lancaster County, in 1979 four farmhands were witness to a very strange entity. At first they assumed the upright creature to be a naked man, but soon realized it was covered in course, light brown hair. The witnesses described the monster's features as "semi-human". The creature was moving through the field in a kangaroo-like series of jumps. One of the witnesses reported that when he got within 100 feet of the entity, he felt a strange sensation, like an electrical shock. The monster turned and shouted something in what seemed like a strange language, then raced into some nearby woods at a pace beyond human ability.

In 1981 another Lancaster County farmer was on his tractor in a field in Drumore Township, when he noticed something red-brown in color lying down. The "something" turned out to be a hair covered biped which stood up when it saw the tractor. The farmer observed the creature walk along the tree line and eventually head into the woods, going in the direction of the Susquehanna River.

Back across the river to York County, in September of 1982, a couple reported seeing a ten foot tall creature. It was 9:00 pm. Coming home from a shopping trip in York, driving on Green Valley Road in Seven Valleys, they witnessed the huge biped cross the road through their high beams. The creature was covered in light brown hair.

The 1990's saw a "gorilla" come back to the Gettysburg area. In 1992 or 1993, a child living outside of Gettysburg heard something he thought was footsteps outside his bedroom window. Looking out he saw a 5½ or six foot tall creature, covered in hair, with broad shoulders and a large head.

A bigfoot creature was spotted very close to York City in 1996. Two men were hunting near the old quarry across from Mt. Rose Cemetery when they felt themselves being hit by small stones. Turning to see who was throwing the rocks, they saw a very tall creature on the hill behind them. The men noticed a smell they likened to sewage. As the witnesses were fleeing, the creature threw a dead tree down the hill toward them.

In 1997 a hunter in Michaux State Forest, Adams County, saw three hair-covered bipedal creatures. One of them was "dragging a baby". A few months later, in January of 1998, a couple driving on Route 116, between Gettysburg and Fairfield, witnessed a bigfoot creature step over a fence then cross the road in two or three big steps.

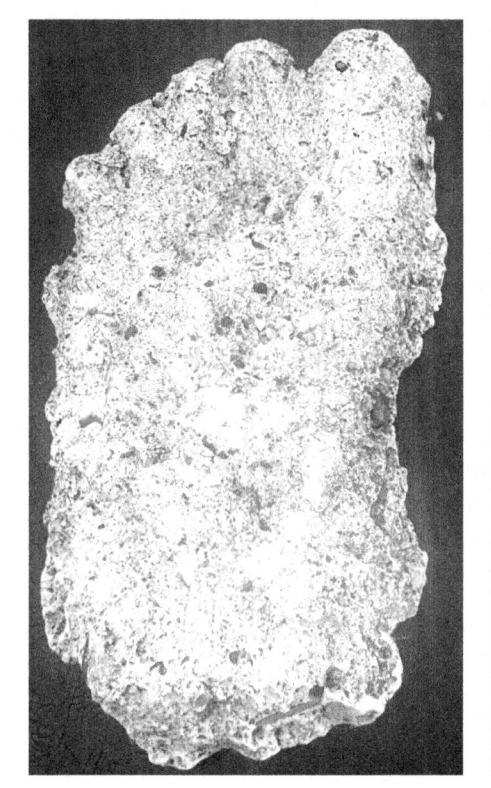

Five-toe and three-toe footprint casts from the collection of Bob Chance. Photographs by Matt Jackson.

We'll go back to Lancaster County to close out the 20th Century. On April 12, 1999, in Honey Brook near Route 10, a man was taking a walk. His attention was drawn by a strange noise. He looked to see a light brown hair-covered creature squatting down and looking at him. The creature stood up, turned, and walked away into the woods on two legs. The witness said the creature was muscular and approximately 7½ feet tall.

In 2001 a strange hairy visitor was coming around a home northeast of Gettysburg in Adams County. On May 15 of that year, the witness saw a six foot tall black creature move behind her garage. She smelled something which she described as rotten fish mixed with garbage. At previous times the witness had noted the plants beneath her bedroom window flattened, as if something had been standing there, looking in the window. She had heard strange noises outside her home at night, and found plants and grass in her yard trampled by an animal of large size. She also noticed branches and twigs broken off of the trees behind her house at about nine feet off the ground. Some twigs were arranged in a circle around one of her trees.

More creepiness came to Chickies Rock area in 2014. On August 25, 2014, a man was fishing in the Chiques Creek, close to where it meets the Susquehanna River. He heard a loud crashing above him. When he went to investigate, he heard another loud crash and a loud growling scream that shook his body. He then left the area. No creature was seen, but the encounter holds many features similar to other bigfoot encounters.

On March 8, 2015, Tom Day saw seventeen inch long tracks in the snow in Newberry Township, York County. The snow was packed hard in each print, as if something very heavy had made the tracks. Some people suggested the tracks could have been left by snowshoes, but there were visible toe prints in the tracks and the stride reached as much as four feet between each print. Tom followed the prints up a hill and down the other side, where the creature appeared to have made a six foot jump down to the road. Tom also reported hearing eerie howls and whoops at night. His neighbors reported seeing large creatures moving through the woods, as well as hearing the whooping sounds and wood knocks. There was also a report of another resident's dog getting beaten up by an "orangutan". Tom found more tracks in 2016 - two sets of prints this time. One of the two sets had a massive 8½ foot stride.

Tracks from Newberry Township. 2015. Photo by Tom Day.

Also in 2015, on June 23, a woman observed a seven to eight foot tall creature covered in dark hair in Willow Street, Lancaster County. She said the creature was swaying back and forth and appeared to be eating something.

I have tried to be as thorough as possible, collecting as many bigfoot sightings as I could find. I am sure I do not have a complete list, but I reported as many as I uncovered. I am sure by the time this book is published I will have found more in the area.

There were other local bigfoot sightings of which I heard tell, but for which I could not find documentation or witnesses. One person remembered a sighting from the 1970's in Seven Valleys, York County, where a chicken house was raided by the creatures. Andrew Gables book, *The Mystery Animals of Pennsylvania,* briefly mentions bigfoot sightings in Hex Hollow, about which I have been able to find no further information. I heard other reports of sightings in southern York County from 2015. I continue to pursue these stories.

Still other York County sightings were in Bob Chance's sightings file, but dates and places were vague:

- A woman from Shrewsbury reported hearing deep squeals and seeing a creature in a cave with large white eyes.

- Raccoon hunters heard screams while night hunting. Their hunting dogs ran back to them - when they turned on their headlamps, the screams stopped.

- A jogger saw the creature in the 1950's on some back roads in the county.

- A biology teacher found tracks with an eight foot stride.

- Tracks were found by hunters in Seven Valleys which, when followed, just stopped in the middle of a field.

I now believe there are far more bigfoot sightings in the area than the ones I have collected. I'm sure many witnesses never come forward for fear they won't be believed or will be ridiculed. Others perhaps report their sightings to the police or the Fish and Game Commission, and these sightings may or may not ever come to public attention.

• • •

15
HEX COUNTRY WEREWOLVES AND BLACK DOGS

When the Germans immigrated to Pennsylvania, it seems they brought with them the werewolves of European legend; for Pennsylvania is known, even today, as a hotbed of werewolf / dogman activity. Native Americans had tales of shape-shifters and werewolf type creatures of their own, long before the Europeans ever landed on these shores. As the Pennsylvania Dutch spread through the eastern and central parts of the state, however, the flavor of stories - along with the werewolf mythology, and the ideas of what these creatures are and how to protect oneself from them - took on a very Germanic form.

There are, in fact, so many werewolf tales in Pennsylvania that we have a term for the ghost of a werewolf: the *spookwolf*. This term is also applied, interchangeably, to the ghost of a wolf - and sometimes to supernatural black dogs, which we shall discuss more later.

In modern times, the werewolf phenomenon seems not so much to manifest in lycanthropy, that is in shape-changing humans who turn into wolves or man-wolf creatures, but rather

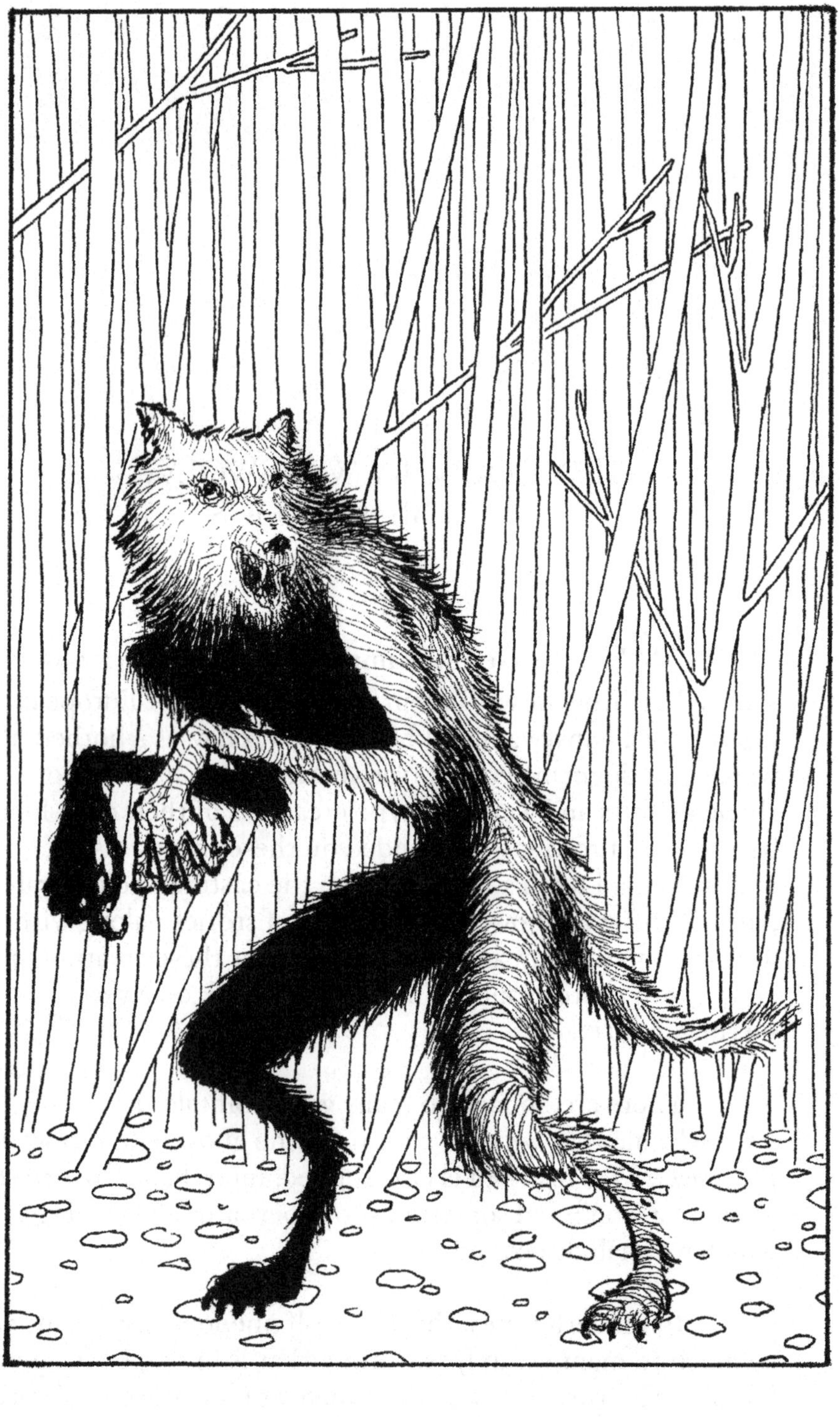

in encounters with the horrible and frightening "dogman", or upright canine. Dogman witness descriptions are remarkably consistent - large (usually six to eight feet tall when standing on two legs), fur covered, muscular, bipedal creatures with clawed hands and wolf-like heads. They are often mistaken for what multiple witnesses describe as "the largest wolf I've ever seen" until they stand up and walk on hind legs. The hind legs are most often described as being crooked, like a dog's legs, with huge canid paws. Another feature expressed almost universally by dogman witnesses is a sense of evil intent about these creatures. Bigfoot witnesses often report a range of reactions upon seeing the creature - from shock and amazement to fear, depending upon the encounter and the demeanor and actions of the creature. However, dogman encounters - even those reported as brief sightings from vehicles - almost always result in a sense of dark dread and shockingly intense fear reported by the witnesses.

Dogman, according to witness reports, seems to be less inclined to hide in the woods and shadows than bigfoot - and although most often reported in forested areas, swamps, and other remote locales, dogmen are also encountered disturbingly close to suburban areas and even cities. In the winter of 2010 a witness' pets started going missing near Jacobus, York County. They subsequently saw a dogman creature in a neighbor's yard.

Weird Pennsylvania has a brief tale of werewolves from the mountains of Adams County in the 1970's. There is little information in the article to go on, other than some rumors. The writer does report a brief sighting of a "huge hairy creature" which leapt across the road in front of the vehicle in which he was traveling. No specific dates or road names are given.

The Google map, *PA Upright Canine / Dogman Witness Sightings*, shows another Adams County dogman encounter. The map briefly details an event from 2015 which took place at a cabin in Michaux State Forest. After hearing noises outside of the cabin throughout the previous night, the witness was chased by a snarling bipedal canine creature.

We go back to Marietta and head just a bit north, to the village of Rowena for another tale of a dogman, werewolves, a white spookwolf, a vampire, and shadow people, all from Hans Graf Cemetery. This small graveyard is notable for the low wall which surrounds all of the graves - yet has no gate.

Hans Graf Cemetery. The wall facing the road bears this legend. [TR]

One tale associated with the cemetery states that a family of German immigrants were accused of being werewolves after moving to Marietta. The entire family of five was shot with silver bullets on the same night, beneath a full moon, and buried within the walls of the cemetery. If this doubtful story were true, then the stones should show the same death date for everyone in the family. A visit to Hans Graf

Cemetery turned up no such group of graves. Perhaps werewolves are buried in unmarked graves? Some say that Hans Graf himself was a werewolf but as Graf is not buried here - only his descendants - it's unclear how or why Hans' spookwolf would prowl these grounds.

Andrew Gable's *The Mystery Animals of Pennsylvania* notes a story regarding Hans Graf Cemetery which will call to mind the Seven Gates of Hell legend from York County, as discussed in earlier chapters. The legend states that if you walk around the perimeter of the cemetery *SEVEN* times under a full moon, then you will die. Another story related by Gable notes that if you walk around the top of the wall which surrounds Hans Graf Cemetery thirteen times, backwards, then a vampire will appear.

Hans Graf Cemetery. 2016. [TR]

Continuing, Gable notes that the most common story associated with the graveyard is that of a ghostly white wolf or white dog seen amongst the graves. Those who do not see the dog are often greeted by a sound of barking which intensifies if one dares to venture over the wall and into the cemetery.

The entry for Hans Graf Cemetery on strangeusa.com notes five shadow people seen by a witness while gazing at the cemetery walls one night - presumably those five lycanthropes whose lives were taken by silver bullets so long ago. The same witness saw a "man-sized wolf" charging on its hind legs down the road from the cemetery.

So many legends from one very small graveyard in a small village out of the way in Lancaster County. It was worth a look. My visit was peaceful enough. I was indeed greeted by the barking of dogs, which seemed however to emanate from neighboring houses, not some otherworld. A small dog seemed to be barking to the northeast (where most of the houses in Rowena lie) and a lower, somewhat more intimidating bark was heard across the fields from the west. Whatever canine issued the second bark, be it natural or supernatural, never approached any closer. I walked around the perimeter, both inside and outside of the walls (alas, not seven times and not under a full moon), taking many photographs. It is a strange little cemetery, but a very interesting one, and pleasing to behold, if you are of the sort that can appreciate such things. As I pulled away after my visit, a black cat immediately crossed the road in front of me.

A somewhat more traditional werewolf tale comes out of York County, with an unspecified date, but believed to be from the 1800's. There was a revival held at the Warrinton Meeting House in Wellsville - the event lasted for several days and nights. Among the people who drifted into the meeting was a strange girl no one seemed to know. She asked to stay a few days with the Ross family, who lived in the area. She ended up staying with the Ross family for several months. At the end of those months, she began to make sounds like a wolf in her sleep. The family began to suspect that she was a *garol,* or werewolf. One night this girl disappeared. She was never seen again. They looked for any sign of her in the area - though there had been rain and the paths were muddy, no human footprints were found. They did, however, find wolf tracks through the woods nearby.

Heading back to Seven Valleys in York County, Lynne Strayer told me a tale of a neighbor who experienced repeated visitations of a black, dog-headed entity. Her neighbor said the creature would stand at the foot of her bed at night. It looked like the Egyptian god, Anubis. At first this tale may seem to fit firmly in the *spookwolf* category (that is to say some sort of spiritual visitation as opposed to a physical creature). However, there have been multiple reports across the country of people waking up to find dogman creatures inside their homes. The possibility of waking up to face a horror like dogman in one's own home is a truly chilling prospect.

The same neighbors reported one night, as they were sitting on their porch, they heard something large pounding through the fields and brush toward them. It sounded "like a herd of buffalo." They never saw what made the frightening sound. They quickly retreated inside rather than face whatever was moving toward them.

Black dogs seem to have a strong folkloric heritage in England, Scotland, and Ireland. There is a very long and detailed history of these ghostly hounds haunting those isles, glaring with glowing, moon-like, or fiery eyes - and often seen as portents of death and other ill omens. Like the unshakable hellhound Robert Johnson sings of, the giant black canines seem to have followed the immigrants from the British Isles to South Central Pennsylvania. One witness reported black dobermans with glowing eyes watching him on Toad Road. Headless hounds and hellhounds are reported at Hex Hollow.

I have collected this strange ghostly tale, which includes a phantom black hound, from *The York Daily* newspaper published on January 20, 1875:

"Spook Story - It is reported that considerable excitement prevails in Heidelberg Township, near Hanover, in regard to "spooks," and there are some startling rumors afloat of terrible ghostly visitations having been seen recently on the York road, close to the Mennonite road. These weird visitants from the other world assume divers forms and shapes, sometimes appearing in the form of a fiery man or child, and again in the shape of a large black dog. Many of the timid absolutely refuse to pass along the haunted spot after nightfall, and the boldest hearts quake and tremble with fear when obliged to pass the vicinity where the "spooks" do nightly congregate and hold their phantom revels."

• • •

16
FLYING PHANTOMS, MOTHMAN, AND THUNDERBIRDS

Native American tribes throughout the continent told tales of giant raptors long before the Europeans ever reached North America. These huge birds of prey, known as thunderbirds, were thought to feed on large mammals. There are even tales of grown men being carried off by the winged things.

The stories seem almost as if they must be some kind of memories passed down from our prehistoric ancestors, except that there are many many modern sightings of massive birds, not just in remote areas of the country, but from right here in Pennsylvania. Most of the sightings seem to come from the Black Forest region of the state, however there have been quite a few sightings in York County.

Many of these sightings were documented by *The York Daily Record* in 2006. On June 12 of that year, at about 10:00 in the morning, Manchester Township resident Pat Grether heard her dog barking and yelping wildly in her back yard. She went out to see what was the matter and immediately laid eyes upon a massive bird. "It looked like a Cadillac," she said. The bird was in a field, separated from her by only a fence.

Grether, who is described in the article as a skeptic and non-drinker, estimated the wingspan of the creature to be 18-to-20 feet. Shaking, and afraid to move, she stood in disbelief as she observed the terrible bird. "Nothing scares me," Grether said, "but this did." Her dog, a chow, not prone to being frightened himself, cowered behind her legs.

Grether described the bird as black, with white feathers at the tips of its wings and a white ring around its neck. She said she was familiar with what eagles and vultures look like, and this bird was neither. She watched in fear for some time until the bird took flight. She said "it's impossible for a bird of that size to be around and nobody else see it."

Somebody else did. In a follow-up article *The York Daily Record* notes about a dozen people calling or emailing to report sightings of the same raptor Grether observed. Don Julius of Washington Township was outside on his family farm when a huge shadow passed over him. He looked up and saw the giant black bird with white markings, as Grether had described. "I never saw anything like it before," Julius said. "I looked up at it, and it kind of circled me, like it was checking me out."

Joann Bollinger was near the Lincoln State Quarry in Thomasville when she saw two huge birds in a field. Juniatta Hall, also of Manchester Township, observed the giant bird from her kitchen window, in a field behind her house. Hall, a bird-watcher, noted, "...it's not something I've ever seen in Pennsylvania. Whatever it was, that bird is not where it's supposed to be."

John Vacero saw the massive raptor swoop to get some roadkill near the Mt. Zion Road and Sherman St intersection (just a few flaps of the wing from Toad Road, as the thunderbird flies). Valero reported via email: "I know I have never seen anything close to its size." He estimated the wingspan to be up to 15 feet in length. Other observers of the giant black bird with white markings guessed the wingspan to be anywhere from eight to twenty feet.

On July 26, 2015, an unnamed witness reported seeing a flying creature near Pinchot Lake dam, York County. Unlike the feathered thunderbirds, this creature's wings were described as bat-like. Its body was four to five feet long with an oval shaped head and a considerable wingspan. Sightings of things which fit the description of prehistoric flying reptiles have been reported all over the world. Add South Central Pennsylvania to the list.

Thunderbirds and possible relic pterosaurs aren't the only flying cryptids seen in the area. Lon Strickler of the website, *Phantoms and Monsters*, has documented ongoing sightings of an entity he has named The Conewago Phantom, but which locals have been calling Old Red Eye. Making its appearance in Adams County, Old Red Eye has been described as a black, winged entity, similar in appearance to the descriptions of West Virginia's Mothman.

Made famous John Keel's book, *The Mothman Prophecies* (later a film of the same name), Mothman is most often associated with Point Pleasant West Virginia. This dark creature has, however, been seen the world over. In West Virginia, sightings of Mothman heralded death and destruction. Keel noted in later years that a disproportionate number of Mothman witnesses die within a year or two of their encounter. In West Virginia of course, the Mothman sightings culminated in a great tragedy - the collapse of the Silver Bridge in 1967, during rush hour. Forty-six people died. Two of the victims were never found. Others have claimed to have seen and even photographed Mothman or similar entities at the location of other grave events - over the cooling towers at Fukushima nuclear power plant, for example, or outside the Twin Towers on 9/11.

But back to South Central PA. Camp Conewago is a boy scout camp located at the Forks - the site where the Little

Conewago stream enters the Big Conewago Creek, just north of New Oxford. This seems to be the center of the Old Red Eye sightings. People had been reporting something fearful around the camp for years - screams and glowing red eyes. Something that frightened them.

Camp Conewago entrance. 2016. Photo by Alison Renner.

In late summer or autumn of 1988, some boy scouts who had been staying at the camp reported hearing crying sounds from the woods. (Note that crying sounds are often reported in association with bigfoot encounters, and also occur in connection with some of our geographic areas of interest, including Toad Road.) The sounds spooked the scouts enough to cause some to break camp and leave early.

Lon Strickler and two friends decided to investigate the strange sounds and camped near the Forks for the weekend. Besides a sensation of being watched and the sound of what may or may not have been footsteps around their camp, the first night passed without incident. On the second evening, however, things began to get strange.

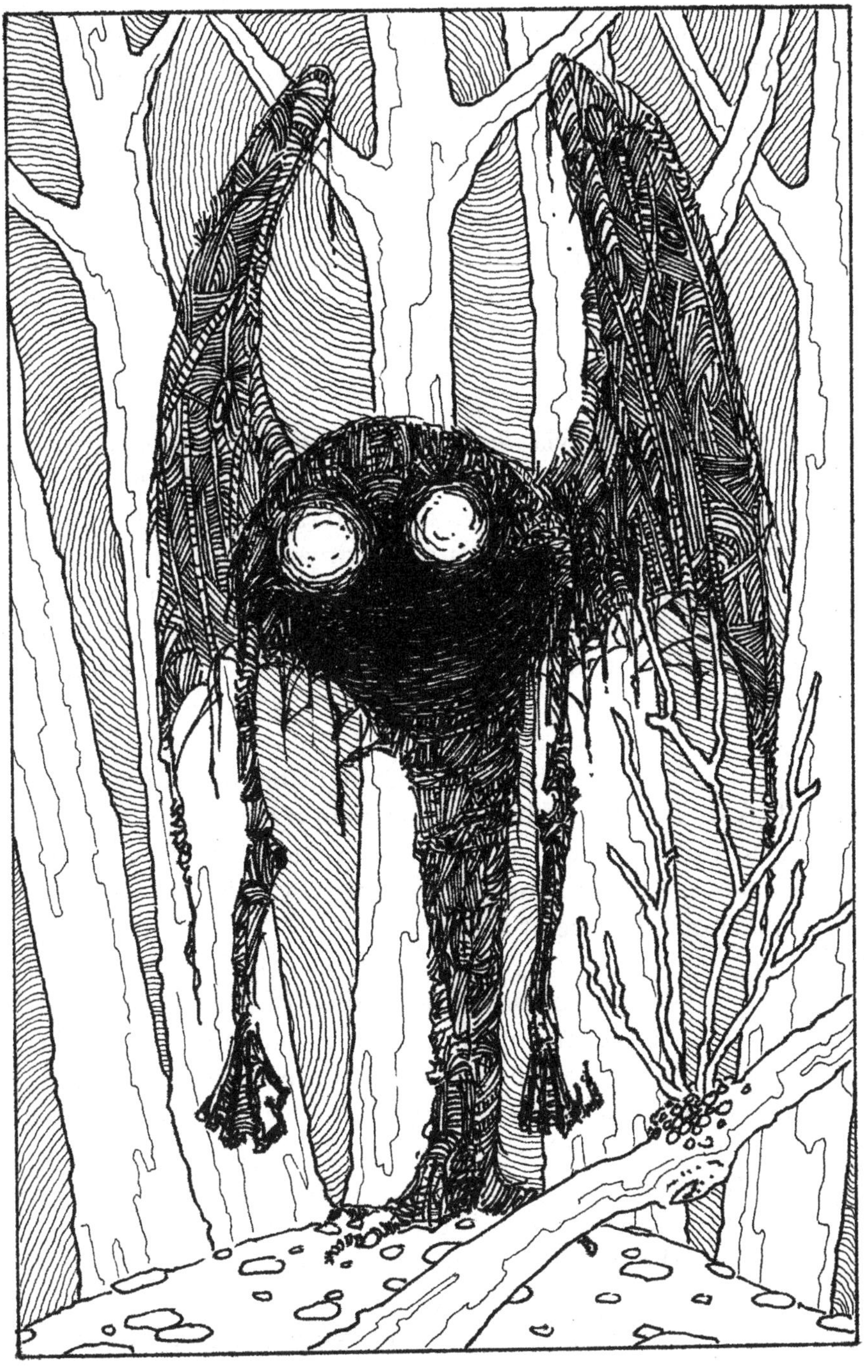

Sitting around the campfire the companions heard something that they at first thought was an owl screeching, but which then started to sound like a child screaming. At about 1:00 am they decided to walk deeper into the woods toward the fork of the creeks. Their attention was drawn to a six foot tall dark figure with glowing red eyes standing in the creek. The entity lifted into the air with a "whoosh" sound and, accompanied by another scream, faded into the distance. Two of the witnesses thought they saw wings or winglike structures protruding from the entity's back.

Strickler (via *Phantoms and Monsters*) has also reported that in 2008 another witness, living near Dick's Dam close to Camp Conewago, contacted him to say that he had often heard the screams in the area. At approximately the same time a boy scout leader reported that his scouts had told him they saw a six foot tall winged "dragon" in the woods at Camp Conewago. They said that the creature appeared to be covered in fur or feathers.

2011 would bring another sighting of Old Red Eye. At dusk on May 8 of that year, a woman traveling on Route 394 saw a large dark creature fly over the bridge as she crossed the Conewago Creek. She said the entity was dark in color, winged, and about the size of a man.

There have also been sightings of what *Phantoms and Monsters* calls a "Mothman-like entity" in Lancaster County. The witness drawing on their website, however, shows something which looks more like the "gargoyles" reported in other parts of the state. These winged entities, unlike Mothman, seem to have a defined head, a visible mouth, pointed ears, and leathery skin. The overall appearance of these creatures has lead witnesses to describe them as living gargoyles.

The Lancaster witness' drawing certainly looks like a gargoyle, showing a fanged, grinning, face and pointed ears. The creature was described as being roughly the size of a man with large "moth-like" wings. Disturbingly, Lancaster's gargoyle was observed floating through the skies, often in daylight, and was seen staring in the windows of witnesses' residences with eerie glowing red eyes. One witness reported that objects inside the home moved on their own during their encounter with the gargoyle entity. The above reports of this gargoyle creature were filed in 2014. The encounters themselves occurred throughout the general Lancaster area starting around 2009.

• • •

17
JERSEY DEVILS, GOATMAN, AND WHAT-IS-ITS

The Jersey Devil, so named for its legendary home in the Pine Barrens of New Jersey, is a very strange creature. It is described as having a horse-like head, an upright body somewhat like that of a kangaroo, and bat-like wings. While most often encountered in its home state, the creature, or others like it, has been reported frequently in Pennsylvania and even as far south as Maryland.

On September 7 of 1910 *The York Daily* announced that The Jersey Devil was seen in York County. William Smuck had seen a strange creature in the area of Springvale which he said was about the size of a shepherd dog but with the legs of a kangaroo. Other witnesses stated that this creature also had quills like a porcupine.

Maryland has, perhaps, the most famous goatman, a creature which indeed bears 'Goatman' as a proper name. Descriptions depict him as a savage Pan-like, axe-wielding satyr - hooved and upright-walking, he is a beheader of family pets and a terrorizor of Prince George's County and surrounding areas. Strange as it may seem, however, goatmen have been reported all over the country. Bearing localized names such as Sheepman, Sheepsquatch, and the Pope Lick Monster, these odd hooved and horned bipeds seem to be haunting the night

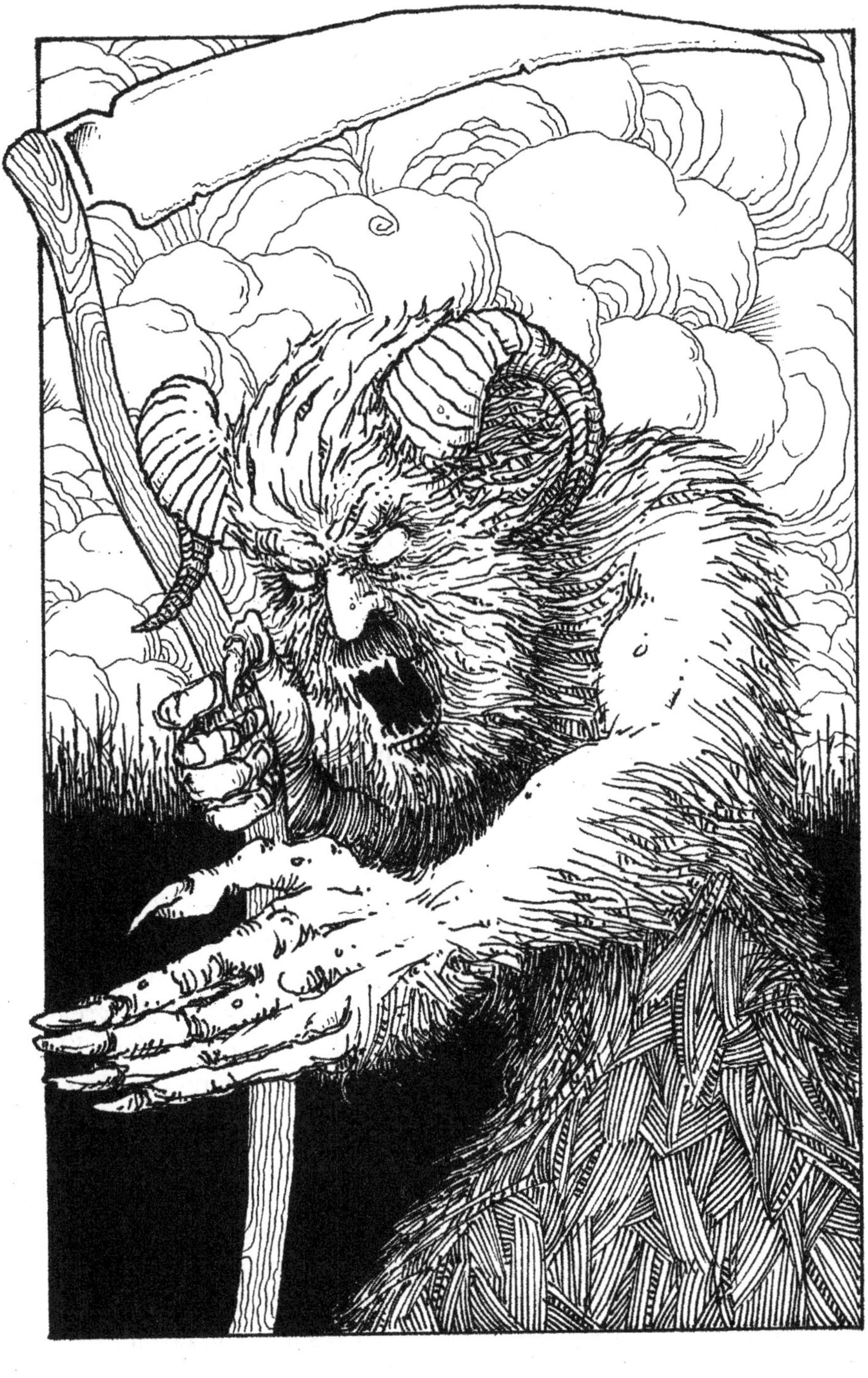

and frightening people in many states. Inconvenient as it is for both hardline skeptics and devoted cryptozoologists alike, the witnesses do insist that these are neither misidentified bears nor bigfoot creatures, but something else entirely.

Legends and theories as to just what goatmen *ARE* vary - from escaped genetic experiments to misidentified relic hominids to satyrs creeping from our collective memory and mythology into the waking world. Who can say for sure? If witnesses are to be believed, however, then *SOMETHING* is out there that is even stranger than bigfoot and dogmen.

Around Erie, PA they have a creature named Sheepman that people have reported seeing since the 1970's. Around six feet tall and bipedal, with sharp claws and ram's horns, the grey hair-covered Sheepman has terrorized teens and late-night drivers throughout the region. It seems the Sheepman, or something very much like him, came to South Central Pennsylvania in 1973.

While Western Pennsylvania was experiencing a wave of UFO and bigfoot creature sightings (see Stan Gordon's *Silent Invasion* for a much more detailed account), something just as strange made its way into Lancaster County in August of 1973.

Two Amish brothers were returning from the fields with a wagon of hay when they saw a creature "the size of a good heifer" with grey hair and a white mane. They said the creature had fangs like a tiger, curved horns like a goat, and claws like a grizzly bear. Their horses bolted in fear, throwing the men to the ground.

The following evening, about 5 miles away, a farmer was clearing weeds with a scythe. Hearing a "ferocious roar", he turned and saw the goatman creature charging. The farmer attempted to defend himself with the scythe, but the creature ripped it from his grasp. Fearing for his life, the farmer fled. Returning the following day, all that was left of the scythe was the blade and the bolts. It appeared as if the creature had eaten the wooden handles and shaft of the scythe.

The goatman's reign of terror continued the following night, on another farm located between the two where the above incidents occurred. A woman was feeding chickens when her attention was drawn by a ruckus near the coop. She saw the goatman grab two geese and make off with them. The woman started after the creature but it turned and threw a goose. The bird hit the woman dead on, with such force that it knocked her to the ground.

P.T. Barnum coined the term What-is-it for his sideshow attractions in the late 19th Century. Since then, the term has been used to describe strange creatures of all stripes. A recent sighting of a unknown animal What-is-it, which happened to be striped, comes to us from York County.

Reported by *Phantoms and Monsters*, in February 2013 a witness was watching television when she caught movement in her back yard. Looking through glass doors, she saw something violently shaking a dogwood tree. After a few moments this creature leapt from the dogwood to a nearby pine tree. The woman only saw the creature briefly, but was sure she had never seen anything of its like in Pennsylvania. She described it as being about four feet in length with grey fur and a long striped tail. The closest comparison from the animal world, said the witness, would be a lemur. She didn't see the creature again but reported hearing scratches on her house beneath her bedroom window on nights following her sighting.

Local business owner, Donald Reeser saw SOMETHING just after midnight in October 2013. Reeser's description somewhat resembles those of the Rake creatures which witnesses across America began reporting around 2008 - feral, skinny humanoid creatures that move like canines. But then again, the face of Reeser's creature looked somewhat like a dogman, but not exactly. A head-scratching What-is-it, to be

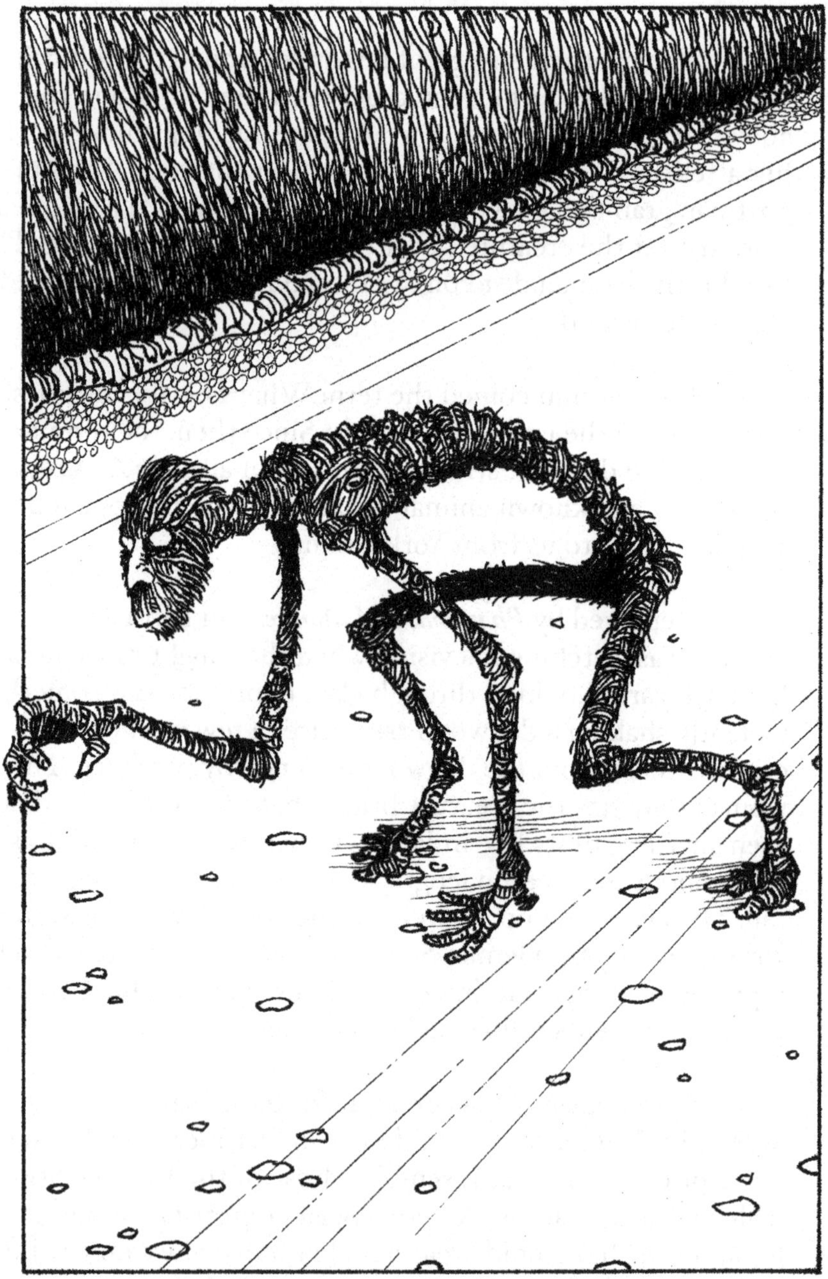

sure, but a frightening one, no less.

According to Reeser's account, he was driving on Route 382 toward Lewisberry, York County. As he neared Brenneman Drive he saw what he assumed to be a very thin, very tall human walking along the roadside. The being appeared to be wearing dark, tight fitting clothing and was walking in an awkward fashion. It was 6½ feet tall, Reeser noted, or perhaps even taller.

The entity moved with what looked like a limping gait, suggesting that the late-night walker may have been in an accident and be in need of assistance. As Reeser approached, it became clear that this was not a human at all. The creature dropped to all fours and scurried with ease across the road. That's when Reeser got a better look at it. It was covered all over with short black hair. Its face was humanoid but with a short dog-like snout, and either it was covered in the same black hair or the creature's skin was black in color as well.

Donald Reeser still doesn't know exactly what he saw, but he's sure it wasn't a bear. After tentatively telling his story to some friends, two other witnesses confessed to Reeser that they had seen something like the creature he saw creeping through the area.

• • •

AFTERWORD: WHAT TO MAKE OF IT ALL

First, I would like to say some words about Nelson D. Rehmeyer. I recently saw the *Hex Hollow* documentary, which does a nice job of covering the events of the "hex murder". In the film, there is a brief reference to *Weird Pennsylvania,* and to my story about Hex Hollow.

My story originally appeared in *Morbid Curiosity* magazine and was heavily edited for the *Weird USA / Weird Pennsylvania* books. I used the same story as the basis for my chapter on Hex Hollow here. If my words in any way suggested to the reader that Nelson Rehmeyer was some kind of sinister figure or a witch of any sort, I apologize sincerely. I did not edit it for the *Weird* books and had no say in how it was printed.

I have made every effort to show that Nelson Rehmeyer was a healer and tried to help his community. I tried to draw distinct lines between powwow and witchcraft, as powwow practitioners would have done in Rehmeyer's time and still do today. Nelson Rehmeyer was the victim of a murder. He was not the sinister one in that horrible situation.

I have attended a lecture by another author who wrote about the Hex Murder. In the speech that I heard, I have to say there was a clear air of: well, Nelson Rehmeyer dabbled with the occult, so he had it coming. Much sympathy was extended toward his murderers, particularly Hess and Curry, but Nelson got none. For my part, I would like to have known Nelson Rehmeyer. I think we would have gotten along quite well. O the stories he could have told me!

As far as spookiness in Rehmeyer's Hollow - I have shown that it was there before the Hex Murder ever happened. Whatever it comes from, I don't think the "hex murder" was the cause of the weirdness in Hex Hollow. It was, perhaps, a side effect or a symptom, but it is not the cause of the strangeness.

I think something else draws the Goblin Universe into Hex Hollow (or vice versa). Perhaps it is Codorus Creek. Perhaps it is something no one can understand. Whatever psychic energy people have invested into the idea of Hex Hollow being full of ghosts and witches has only added to the aura of weird.

• • •

Are there monsters prowling our fields and forests? Are ghosts singing in our cemeteries? Are orbs and mists following us through the park? Many witnesses say yes.

Are these things flesh and blood creatures or are they, like the Seven Gates of Hell themselves, only some kind of imagined thing made real or semi-real by some process beyond our understanding?

Bigfoot creatures, which appear again and again throughout this book, are the most commonly encountered cryptid. They are also the most man-like. Some Native American traditions hold them as people, not animals, and many who have researched the phenomenon agree. Do we see bigfoot more often because they are so much like us - or do we tend to make our monsters in our own reflection?

When I started running into so many bigfoot sightings in South Central Pennsylvania, I was surprised. How could this be? The area simply isn't that remote. As I talked to people who had studied bigfoot for far longer than I, I was told again and again that this is somewhat common. This is a species that has coexisted with us for centuries, and they have learned more about us than we have learned about them. Bigfoot can see better than us at night; they probably hear better; they are faster, and stronger, and know the woods better than we could ever hope to. Bigfoot are also masters at hiding and using natural camouflage. *Survivorman* Les Stroud has put forth the idea that bigfoot could have savant-like abilities to hide themselves.

If all of that is the case, perhaps they are natural animals. Perhaps we've walked by them in the woods and never even realized it. If they are natural animals - and especially if they are ones with natural abilities that appear to be far beyond those of humans - then why not live close to us? Close to our farms and orchards, whee food is readily available?

Perhaps, however, this mysterious closeness is just one aspect of a wider problem, one that many bigfoot researchers don't like to discuss because it starts putting question marks all around the "undiscovered ape in the woods" theory of bigfoot. The problem is: where bigfoot goes, other strange things follow. Or vice versa.

Stan Gordon devoted an entire book, *Silent Invasion*, to documenting the connection between bigfoot creatures and UFOs in Pennsylvania alone. Even Stan hadn't noted the UFO and bigfoot sightings around Peach Bottom/Delta/Fawn Grove in 1978. I found separate newspaper articles from the time mentioning the incidents. I was not terribly surprised.

It's confusing and it's bizarre, but where bigfoot goes, so go UFOs, orbs, mists, ghosts, and other strange things. They just seem to happen in the same places, around the same time. Not always, but often enough.

Of course, the questions extend beyond bigfoot and into even stranger things like dogmen and goatmen. These are things that science says simply cannot exist. Yet people report them. Dependable witnesses with nothing to gain give detailed reports and descriptions.

What about the places? Hex Hollow. Toad Road. Chickies Rock. Hans Graf Cemetery. Why is so much weirdness focused on certain places? Why do certain places give people " that feeling" of creepiness or of the OTHER? Why are so many of these things reported near the river or various creeks? What about the iron furnaces?

Some researchers believe that what separates us from other dimensions is a thin magnetic field of some sort. If magnetic fields are involved, it may stand to reason that places where iron was processed, like furnaces, would become part of the mystery. It is also noted that places where quartz is naturally plentiful seem to have more paranormal activity. The Hellam Hills / Toad Road area certainly fits that description, as do other areas of interest covered in this book.

At present all of these theories remain theories. Perhaps one day science will catch up to the paranormal. However, I think the inhabitants of the Goblin Universe - or whatever trickster agency it is that controls them - will always be able to keep one step ahead of us. If that step leaves a footprint, we can study it and cast it and try to figure out what it was that left it, but we may be left with just a footprint.

I'm afraid there will always be more questions than answers. For my part I can only say I think the world is far stranger than we could ever grasp. I think the nights are darker than we remember from the safety of our comfortable couches, warm behind locked doors. Engrossed by the all-too-real human monsters which dominate our 24-hour news cycle, we've forgotten those older monsters which stalk us in the forest and shriek from the shadows. We've placed them on the bookshelf in tomes of folklore and mythology. Yet even if we have forgotten them, I don't think those old monsters have forgotten us.

• • •

APPENDIX I:
BIGFOOT AND OTHER CRYPTID SIGHTINGS AND SIGNS BY DATE
(IN ADAMS, YORK, AND LANCASTER COUNTIES)

- December, 1858. Lancaster, Lancaster County. "Wild-man" sighting reported - multiple witnesses report seeing "a thing like a man, but hairy like a bear." (via *Strange Pennsylvania Monsters*)

- August, 1871. Welsh Mountain, Lancaster County. "Hairy man" reported in area. (via *Strange Pennsylvania Monsters*)

- December 6, 1872. Bottstown, York County. "Wild man" spotted. (via *The York Daily*)

- August 1874. Saeger's Woods, near Hanover, York County. A masked "wild man" wearing woman's clothes witnessed on multiple occasions, being followed by a black dog. (via *The York Daily*) - note: probably not a cryptid, but this was too wonderfully crazy a sighting not to include!

- September, 1874. Near Morgantown, Lancaster County.
A "wild man of immense stature and terrible aspect" is reported in the area, at this time every year. (via *Reading Times*)

- March, 1883. Hanover, York County.
Something described as having the dual form of a man and a bear was stalking the streets of Hanover at night. (via *Hanover Spectator*)

- Late October 1886. Delta, York County.
A group of people encounter a 12-15 foot high "monster" when returning from evening church services. (via *The Delta Herald*)

- September 7, 1910. Springvale, York County.
Man sees "Jersey Devil" creature.

- 1912. Kinderhook, Lancaster County.
Sighting of "wild-man" reported. (via *Strange Pennsylvania Monsters*)

- January 20, 1921. Idaville, Adams County.
Residents give chase to "huge gorilla." (via *The Gettysburg Times*)

- August, 1921. Gettysburg, Adams County.
Multiple witnesses report seeing a "gorilla" on York Street. (via *The Gettysburg Times*)

- August, 1921. York Springs, Adams County. Gardners, Adams County.
"Gettysburg Gorilla" creature reported throughout the area. (via *The Gettysburg Times*)

- August 21, 1921. Near Fairfield, Adams County.
Five foot tall, upright-walking, hairy creature crosses road in front of witness. (via *The Gettysburg Times*)

- 1950's. York County.
  Jogger reports seeing creature on back roads. (via Bob Chance bigfoot sighting files)

- 1957. Near Hanover, York County.
  Woman parked in a wooded area south of Hanover is approached by bigfoot creature. (via *The Gettysburg Times*)

- July 1, 1961. Near Emmitsburg Road as it crosses Marsh Creek, Adams County.
  Five foot tall long-haired creature encountered in woods. (via *Mystery Animals of Pennsylvania*)

- 1965. Tolna, York County.
  Nighttime jogger sees bigfoot creature cross the road. (via Bob Chance bigfoot sighting files)

- 1967-1968. "Gorilla" reported outside of Glen Rock, PA.
  Thought to be responsible for livestock deaths. (via Bob Chance bigfoot sighting files)

- 1970's. Werewolves reported in the mountains of Adams County. No further information given. (via *Weird Pennsylvania*)

- 1972. Near Muddy Creek, York County.
  Ecology teacher Bob Chance and a group of students encounter possible bigfoot creature. (via *York Daily Record*)

- 1972 or 1973. Manchester Township, York County.
  Loud breaking branches and a loud "inhuman" shriek heard by campers. (via BFRO)

- August, 1973. Lancaster County.
  Two Amish men witness an upright-walking hair-covered goatman type creature. (via *Silent Invasion*)

- August, 1973. Lancaster County.
  On the evening following the above report, a farmer is

attacked by the same or a similar goatman creature. (via *Silent Invasion*)

- 1973. Near Lancaster, Lancaster County.
Woman chases goatman creature after it steals two geese. (via *Silent Invasion*)

- December 1, 1973. Hellam Township, York County.
Man hospitalized after being attacked by "green haired monster" on Trout Run Road (near Toad Road). (via *York Daily Record*)

- 1973-1976. Peach Bottom, Delta, York County.
Repeated sightings of seven foot tall, hair covered, bigfoot-like entities in the woods. (via BFRO)

- April 24, 1975. South of Fawn Grove, York County.
Motorist hits bigfoot creature. (via *The Gettysburg Times*)

- 1975. Delta, York County.
Family reports hearing howls and having many other encounters with bigfoot creature. (via Bob Chance bigfoot sighting files)

- January 10, 1978. Near Fawn Grove, York County.
Witness reports seeing a ten foot tall biped with shining white eyes. (via *The Gettysburg Times*)

- January 28, 1978. Delta, York County.
Allen Hilsmier finds large 16-inch tracks with a five foot stride in the snow on his farm. (via *The Gettysburg Times*)

- February 13, 1978.
On a farm about ten miles away from the Hilsmeier farm, 30 chickens were killed. Large tracks lead to and from the coop.

- March 2, 1978. Near Peach Bottom, York County.
Witness spots seven foot tall creature near Peach Bottom

Power Plant. Security guards report hearing screams and find large footprints. (via *York Daily Record*)

- Early March, 1978. Near Spring Grove, York County.
Motorist sees bigfoot creature and police find tracks. (via *Strange Pennsylvania Monsters*)

- September, 1978. Gifford Pinchot State Park, York County.
The wall of a camper was hit by unknown being at 2:00 am. (via PA Bigfoot Society)

- November 27, 1978. Near Holtwood Dam, York County.
Hunter is paced by creature in the woods, then observes a seven foot tall creature. (via *York Daily Record*)

- 1979. Lancaster County.
Four farmhands spot a strange, upright creature covered in light colored hair, and hopping across a field. (via *Strange Pennsylvania Monsters*)

- Fall, 1981. Drumore Township, Lancaster County.
A man on a tractor witnesses a reddish-brown creature. (via PA Bigfoot Society)

- September, 1982. Seven Valleys, York County.
Husband and wife observe a ten foot tall, bipedal, light brown colored creature cross the road in front of their vehicle. (via *The Bigfoot Phenomenon in Pennsylvania*)

- Early Fall, 1988. Camp Conewago, Adams County.
Witnesses hear what sounds like children crying in the woods, then observe a dark figure, possibly winged, with glowing red eyes. (via *Phantoms and Monsters*)

- 1992 or 1993. Near Gettysburg, Adams County.
A child hears footsteps outside and observes a hair-covered creature. (via *Strange Pennsylvania Monsters*)

- February 11, 1994. Near Quarryville, Lancaster County.
16" long human-like footprints with a four foot stride found in snow. (via BFRO)

- June 1997. Michaux State Forest, Adams County.
Witness hears howls similar to howler monkeys, but much longer and more intense. (via Pennsylvania Research Organization)

- 1996. Springettsbury Township, York County.
Two men encounter bigfoot creature near old quarry. (via author interview with witness)

- Late October, 1997. Michaux State Forest, Adams County.
A hunter witnesses three bigfoot creatures - including a juvenile. (via *Strange Pennsylvania Monsters*)

- January, 1998. Route 116 between Fairfield and Gettysburg, Adams County.
Witnesses in vehicle see bigfoot step over a fence and cross the road. (via *Strange Pennsylvania Monsters*)

- April 12, 1999. Near Honey Brook, Lancaster County.
Witness observes 7½ foot tall muscular creature, covered in dark brown hair. (via PA Bigfoot Society)

- 2000. Pinkerton Road, Lancaster County.
A group of friends witness five foot tall hair-covered albatwitch creature cross road in front of their car. (via *Ghosts of the River Towns*)

- May 15, 2001. Near Route 15, northeast of Gettysburg, Adams County.
Witness sees black, six foot tall creature move behind her garage. (via Bigfoot Encounters)

- November / December 2001. Near Goldsboro, York County.
12-to-15 inch footprint found. (via PA Bigfoot Society)

- February, 2002. Near Marietta, Lancaster County.
  Rick Fisher witnesses skinny, bi-pedal albatwitch creature, about four-to-five feet tall, covered with black hair. (via Rick Fisher / *Ghosts of the River Towns*)

- February 14, 2002. Waynesboro Rervoir, Adams County.
  Creature footprints found along creek bed. (via *Mystery Animals of Pennsylvania*)

- September 9, 2004. Lititz, Lancaster County.
  Man "call blasts" reported bigfoot sounds (taken from a television program) into woods behind his home. Several gutteral screams were heard in reply. (via PA Bigfoot Society)

- June 12, 2006. Manchester Township, York County.
  Woman reports sighting of huge unknown bird with 18-20 foot wingspan behind her house. Several other witnesses in the county would report seeing similar massive birds around this time. (via *York Daily Record*)

- 2008. Near Dick's Dam, Adams County.
  Man claims that for many years he has heard screams similar to those reported from the Conewago Phantom / Old Red Eye. (via *Phantoms and Monsters*)

- 2008. Camp Conewago, Adams County.
  Boy Scouts report seeing a six foot tall, fur or feather-covered "dragon" in the woods. (via *Phantoms and Monsters*)

- July 18, 2008. Near Red Lion, York County.
  Witness observes a short, grey-haired, albatwitch-like entity running upright through a field. (via *Phantoms and Monsters*)

- Winter 2010. Near Jacobus, York County.
  Dogman creature witnessed. (via Pennsylvania Upright Canine Witness Sighting Report Locations map on google maps)

- May 8, 2011. Route 394 bridge at Conewago Creek, Adams County.
  Witness observes a dark, winged creature, the size of a full grown man, fly over the bridge in front of her. (via *Phantoms and Monsters*)

- October 2013. Lewisberry, York County.
  Man observes a strange, skinny, upright-walking entity covered in black hair that dropped to all fours and scurried across the road in front of his car.

- August 25, 2014. Chiques Creek, near the Susquehanna River, Lancaster County.
  Fisherman hears loud crashing in the woods, and hears growl / scream. (via PA Bigfoot Society)

- March 8, 2015. Newberry Township, York County.
  Large tracks found in snow. Whoops and wood knocks heard from woods. (via *York Daily Record* / PA Bigfoot Society)

- June 23, 2015. Willow Street, Lancaster County.
  seven-to-eight foot tall dark haired creature observed. (via PA Bigfoot Society)

- July 26, 2015. Pinchot Lake dam, York County.
  Large bat-winged pterosaur-like creature sighted.

APPENDIX II:
MAPS

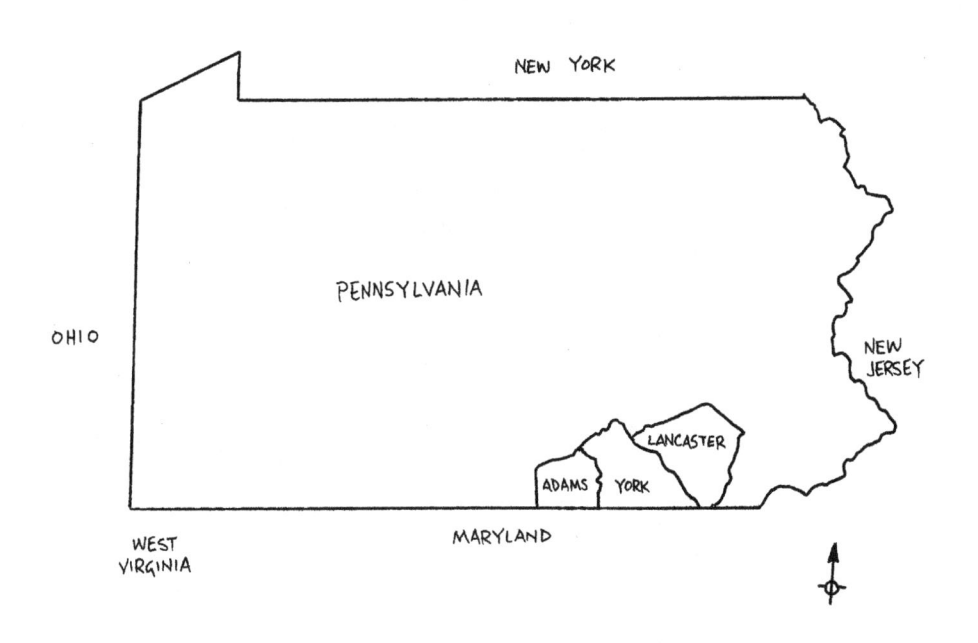

Map I: Pennsylvania and our areas of interest

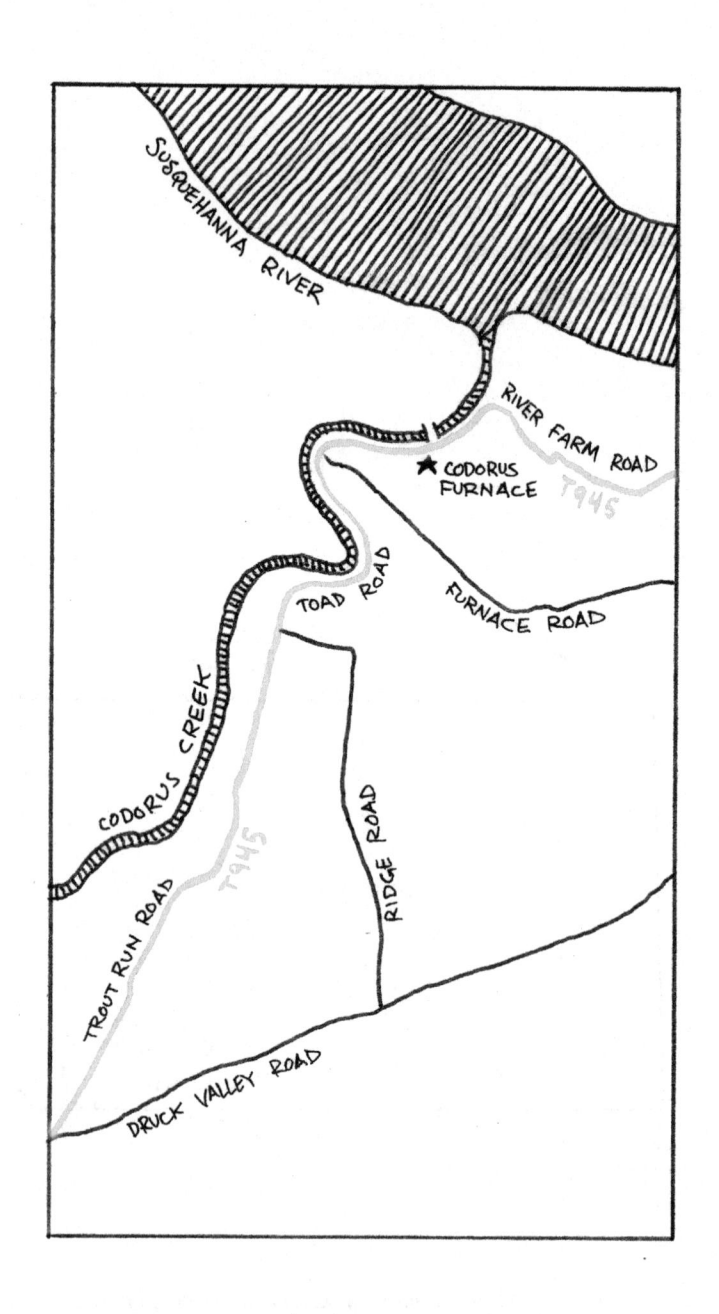

Map II: Toad Road (in grey) as it was before 1945. Furnace Road ended at Toad Road.

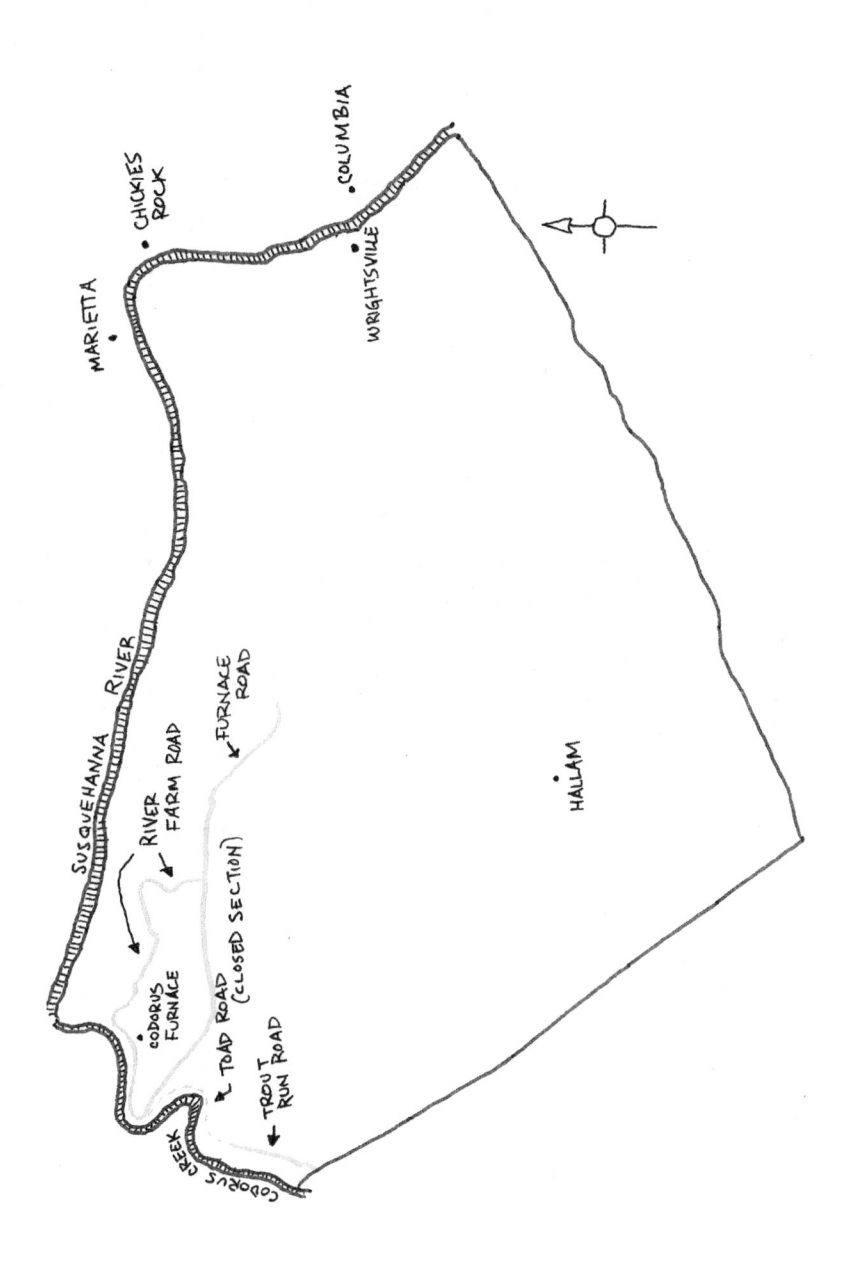

MAP III: Hellam Township and Toad Road as it is today.

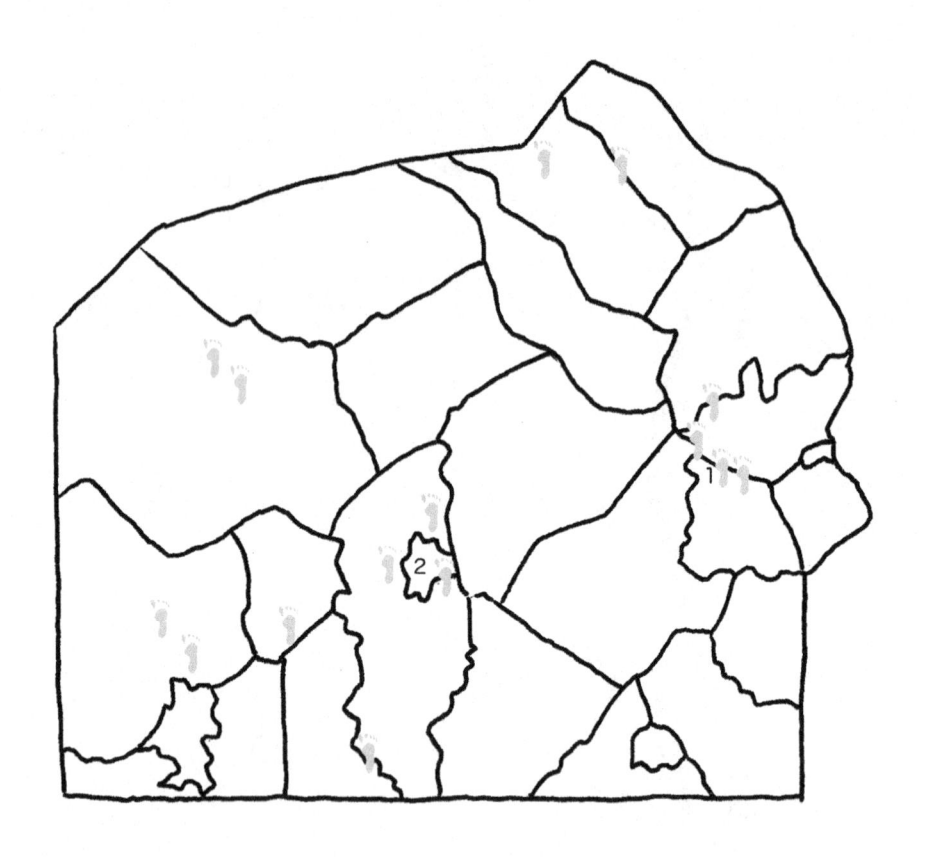

Map IV: Adams County

1 = Camp Conewago

2 = Gettysburg

Footprints indicate approximate locations of cryptid sightings.

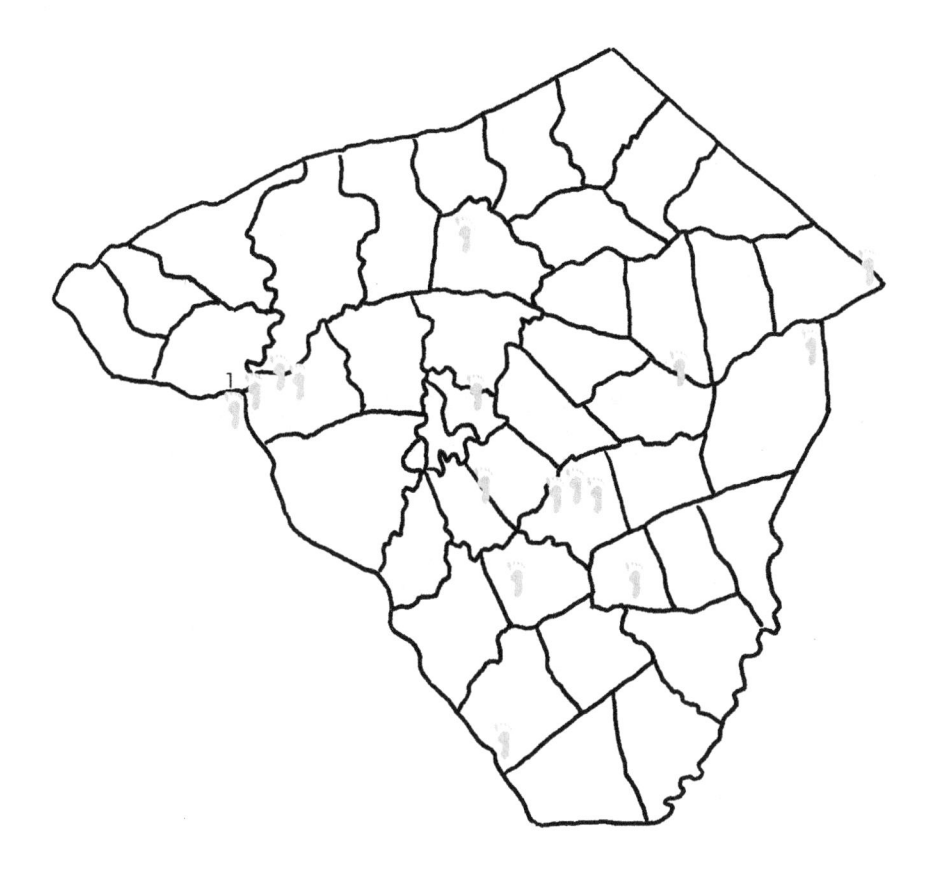

Map V: Lancaster County

1 = Chickies Rock area

Footprints indicate approximate locations of cryptid sightings.

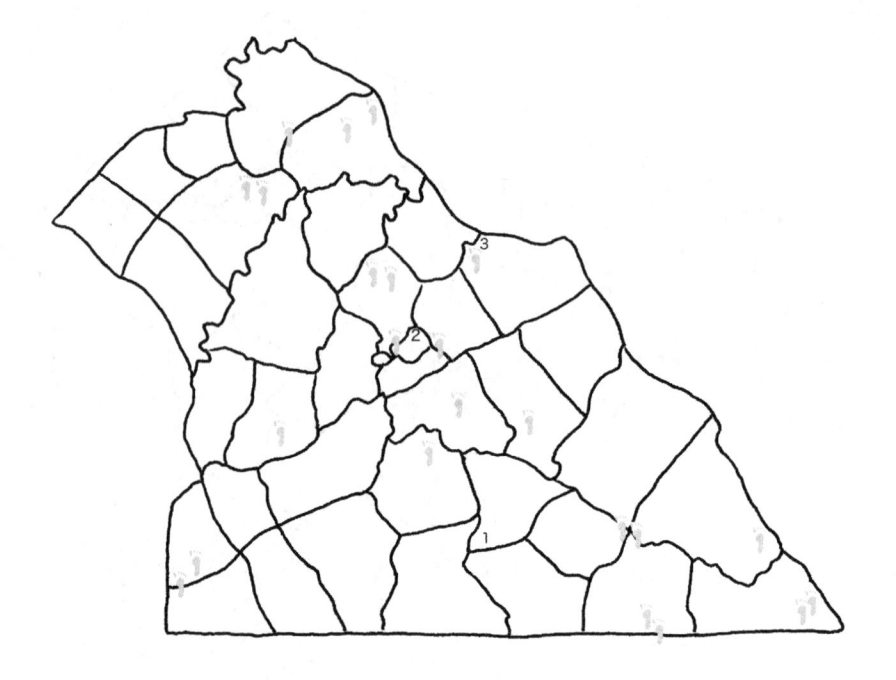

Map VI: York County

1 = Rehmeyer's Hollow area

2 = York City

3 = Toad Road / Codorus Furnace area

Footprints indicate approximate locations of cryptid sightings.

BIBLIOGRAPHY

- Adams, Charles J. III. *Pennsylvania Dutch Country Ghosts Legends and Lore*. (Exeter House Books, 1994)
- Butcher, Scott D. and Dinah Roseberry. *Spooky York Pennsylvania*. (Schiffer Publishing, Ltd., 2008)
- Chance, Bob. *Earthline*. (Coachwhip Publications, 2008)
- Chance, Bob. Bigfoot Sighting Report Files.
- Couch, J. Nathan. *Goatman: Flesh or Folklore*. (J. Nathan Couch, 2014)
- *Daily Capital Journal*. "Lectures Ended". Salem, Oregon: *Daily Capital Journal*, June 14, 1927.
- *The Delta Herald*. "A Ghost Story". Delta, Pennsylvania: The Delta Herald, November 5, 1886.
- Diehl, Catherine. Interview with Phillip Smith. Audio cassette. Private collection of the author.
- *The Evening News*
    "Persons and Incidents Figuring in Witch Doctor Murder in York County". Harrisburg, Pennsylvania: The Evening News, December 1, 1928.
    "Mother of Blymire Believes He Was Hexed". Harrisburg, Pennsylvania: The Evening News, January 10, 1929.
- *The Evening Sun* "Claims UFO Sighting". Hanover, Pennsylvania: The Evening Sun, October 29, 1973.
- Fiedel, Dorothy Butz. *Haunted Lancaster County Pennsylvania*. (Dorothy Burtz Fiedel, 1994)
- Fisher, Rick. *Ghosts of the River Towns*. (Fisher Productions, 2006)
- Frazier, Jeffrey R.

- *Pennsylvania Fireside Tales, Vol. III*. (Egg Hill Publications, 2000)
- *Pennsylvania Fireside Tales, Vol. IV*. (Egg Hill Publications, 2001)
- Gable, Andrew. *The Mystery Animals of Pennsylvania*. (CFZ Press, 2012)
- *The Gazette and Daily*.

  "Doctor Belknap, Who was in Last War, Again Answers Call". York, Pennsylvania: The Gazette and Daily, October 8, 1942.

  "Transferred - Captain Harold P. Belknap...". York, Pennsylvania: The Gazette and Daily, July 3, 1943.

  "York Medical Club Meeting". York, Pennsylvania: The Gazette and Daily, May 28, 1934.
- *The Gettysburg Times*.

  "Gorilla Story No Longer a Myth". Gettysburg, Pennsylvania: The Gettysburg Times, January 21, 1921.

  "Gorilla Was a Mule". Gettysburg, Pennsylvania: The Gettysburg Times, January 25, 1921.

  "See 'Gorilla' Again". Gettysburg, Pennsylvania: The Gettysburg Times, January 27, 1921.

  "Chase Gorilla to Mountains". Gettysburg, Pennsylvania: The Gettysburg Times, January 28, 1921.

  "Town Residents See 'Gorilla'". Gettysburg, Pennsylvania: The Gettysburg Times, August 9, 1921.

  "Only Original Gorilla Seen in County Again". Gettysburg, Pennsylvania: The Gettysburg Times, August 24, 1921.

  "Harrisburg Has Rash of UFO Reports". Gettysburg, Pennsylvania: The Gettysburg Times, August 2, 1967.

  "Big Foot on Visit?". Gettysburg, Pennsylvania: The Gettysburg Times, February 23, 1978.

"Sasquatch Visited Hanover?" .Gettysburg, Pennsylvania: The Gettysburg Times, February 27, 1978.

"York Lists Sightings of UFOs". Gettysburg, Pennsylvania: The Gettysburg Times, April 10, 1978.

"Driving Points for Tourists, Part II". Gettysburg, Pennsylvania: The Gettysburg Times, March 23, 1989.

- Gordon, Stan. *Silent Invasion: The Pennsylvania UFO-Bigfoot Casebook.* (Stan Gordon, 2010)
- *Hanover Spectator*. "A Spook". Hanover, Pennsylvania: Hanover Spectator, March 28, 1883.
- *Harrisburg Telegraph*.

"Another Tradition Destroyed". Harrisburg, Pennsylvania: Harrisburg Telegraph, April 2, 1903.

"Codorus Charcoal Furnace, Revolutionary Landmark, Abandoned 65 Years Ago". Harrisburg, Pennsylvania: Harrisburg Telegraph, February 20, 1915.

"Indians of Dauphin and Lancaster Fought for Land". Harrisburg, Pennsylvania: Harrisburg Telegraph, July 20, 1915.

- Hartman, Don. *Bottles & Jugs with a York, Pennsylvania Perspective.* (W.F.O. Rosenmiller, 1998)
- Hohman, John George. *Pow-Wows or The Long Lost Friend.* (Buzzards' Nob Press, 1976) - reprint of book first published in 1819.
- *Indiana Gazette*. "Historians Compile A List of Mysteriously Missing". Indiana, Pennsylvania: The Indiana Gazette, January 14, 1952.
- Johnson, Paul G. *The Bigfoot Phenomenon in Pennsylvania.* (Paul G. Johnson, 2007)
- Lake, Matt (editor). *Weird Pennsylvania.* (Sterling Publishing, 2007)
- Lewis, Arthur H. *Hex.* (Trident Press, 1969)
- Motter, Leo. *Haunted Places in York County Pennsylvania* (Example Product Manufacturer, 2005)

- *MUFON UFO Journal* #118, September 1977. (Mutual UFO Network, Inc.)
- Napier, John. *Bigfoot: The Yeti and Sasquatch in Myth and Reality.* (E.P. Dutton & Co., 1973)
- *Newsweek Special Edition: Bigfoot.* (Topix Media Specials, 2015)
- *The New York Times.* "Another Pennsylvania Story." New York, New York: The New York Times, January 31, 1878.
- *The News-Herald.* "Flying Saucers in Pennsylvania". Franklin, Pennsylvania: The News-Herald, July 9, 1947.
- Newton, Michael. *Strange Pennsylvania Monsters.* (Schiffer Publishing, 2012)
- *Observer-Reporter.* "Camping in State? Beware of Bigfoot". Washington, Pennsylvania: Observer-Reporter, August 3, 1978.
- Paulides, David.
  >*Missing 411: the Devil's in the Details.* (CreateSpace Independent Publishing Platform, 2014)
  >*Missing 411: Eastern United States.* (CreateSpace, 2011)
- *Reading Times.* "The Wild Man, the Wild Beast, and the Big Snake". Reading, Pennsylvania: Reading Times, September 22, 1874.
- Rosenberger, Homer Tope. *Mountain Folks.* (Annie Halenbake Ross Library, 1974)
- *The St. Louis Republic.* "Ghost in Black Haunts Pennsylvania Cemetery". St. Louis, Missouri: The St. Louis Republic, April 6, 1902.
- *The Sunday News.* "Invaders Hunted 'Munitions Plant' Buried Deep in York County Woods". Lancaster, Pennsylvania: The Sunday News, September 14, 1947.
- *The White Rose Motorist.* "Codorus Forge". York, Pennsylvania: The White Rose Motorist, January, 1935.
- Wilson, Patty A. *Monsters of Pennsylvania.* (Stackpole Books, 2010)
- *The York Daily.*
  >Page 1. York, Pennsylvania: The York Daily, December 10, 1872.
  >"A Wild Man". York, Pennsylvania: The York Daily, August 11, 1874.

"Spook Story". York, Pennsylvania: The York Daily, January 20, 1875.
"Lehmeyer (sic) Valley Jottings". York Pennsylvania: The York Daily, September 10, 1891.
"Rehmeyer's Valley Jottings". York Pennsylvania: The York Daily, July 21, 1892.
"Rehmeyer Valley". York Pennsylvania: The York Daily, August 25, 1892.
"Jersey Devil in County". York, Pennsylvania: The York Daily, September 8, 1910.

- *York Daily Record*.
"Club Seeks Treasurer's Ouster". York, Pennsylvania: York Daily Record, February 11, 1971.
"County Woman Seeks Identity of UFO". York, Pennsylvania: York Daily Record, February 22, 1973.
"UFOs Seen Here Twice". York, Pennsylvania: York Daily Record, October 15, 1973.
"More UFOs Sighted Here." York, Pennsylvania: York Daily Record, October 16, 1973.
"'Blimp-Like' UFO Spotted". York Pennsylvania: York Daily Record, October 23, 1973.
"Monster Not Found". York, Pennsylvania: York Daily Record, December 4, 1973.
"UFO Sighted". York, Pennsylvania: York Daily Record, February 11, 1975.
"Woods Fires Extinguished". York, Pennsylvania: York Daily Record, April 22, 1977.
"UFO Corn Roast?". York, Pennsylvania: York Daily Record, November 4, 1977.
"Bigfoot 'Wild Man of Woods' Roams County". York, Pennsylvania: York Daily Record, February 23, 1978.
"Bigfoot: Baltimore Trucker Sees Seven-Foot 'Whopper' Near Atomic Plant". York, Pennsylvania: York Daily Record, March 7, 1978.

"Stalking Bigfoot: Pair Study Sightings". York, Pennsylvania: York Daily Record January 15, 1979.
"Huge, Scary Bird Sighting". York, Pennsylvania: York Daily Record, June 19, 2006.
"Residents Continue Spotting Big Bird". York, Pennsylvania: York Daily Record, June 23, 2006.
"Does Bigfoot Stalk Northern York County?". York, Pennsylvania: York Daily Record, March 13, 2015.

Websites:

- Bigfoot Encounters - state by state sightings
    bigfootencounters.com

- Bigfoot Field Researchers Organization (BFRO) - sightings by region
    bfro.net

- Google Maps - *PA Upright Canine / Dogman Witness Sightings Map*

- Lancaster Online
    lancasteronline.com *Chickies Rock Tour Offers a Creepy Glimpse of the Past*

- Pennsylvania Bigfoot Society
    pabigfootsociety.com/recent-reports.htm

- Pennsylvania Research Organization
    paresearchers.com

- Phantoms and Monsters

phantomsandmonsters.com/2011/05/new-sighting-of-conewago-phantom.html

phantomsandmonsters.com/2011/10/murder-in-rehmeyer-hollow.html

phantomsandmonsters.com/2013/02/odd-sighting-in-york-county-pa.html

phantomsandmonsters.com/2013/06/just-facts-johnny-depp-as-alf-ufo-light.html

SEEKERS :
CRYPTID RESEARCH IN SOUTH CENTRAL PENNSYLVANIA AND BEYOND

Report a sighting!

If you have seen bigfoot, dogman, or other strange creatures please contact our investigation team, Seekers. We are located in York County but we will travel as needed. Investigation, documentation, and consultation. Free and confidential - we will not use your name or give your exact location without your permission.

Call or text any time and leave a message: 717-347-8554
We will get back to you as soon as possible.

or go to:

seekerspa.blogspot.com

THE ALBATWITCH
PENNSYLVANIA'S LITTLE BIGFOOT

"The Albatwitch: Pennsylvania's Little Bigfoot"
t-shirts, prints, and other cryptid gear available.
Contact the author for more information.

ABOUT THE AUTHOR

Timothy Renner has written articles for several publications including *Morbid Curiosity*, *Weird USA*, and *Weird Pennsylvania*. His illustrations have appeared in fanzines, comics, magazines, books, and on many record covers. Timothy plays and sings folk music with his band Stone Breath. To date they have released twelve full length albums and multiple EPs.
Beyond the Seventh Gate is his first book.

Contact Timothy via email: TimeMothEye@gmail.com

Author photo by Danielle Yagodich.

Made in the USA
Middletown, DE
02 April 2023